# TIBET
Through
Dissident
Chinese Eyes

# TIBET
## Through
# Dissident Chinese Eyes

*Essays on Self-Determination*

Edited by
Cao Changching
and James D. Seymour

An East Gate Book

*M.E. Sharpe*
Armonk, New York
London, England

**An East Gate Book**

Copyright © 1998 by M. E. Sharpe, Inc.

All rights reserved. No part of this book may be reproduced in any form without written permission from the publisher, M. E. Sharpe, Inc., 80 Business Park Drive, Armonk, New York 10504.

Eight of the essays that appear in this volume were originally published in *Chinese Studies in History: A Journal of Translations*, Vol. 30, No. 3 (Spring 1997).

**Library of Congress Cataloging-in-Publication Data**

Tibet through dissident Chinese eyes : essays on self-determination / edited by Cao Chang-ching and James D. Seymour.
    p. cm.
"An East gate book"
Includes bibliographical references and index.
ISBN 1-56324-922-7 (c); ISBN 1-56324-923-5 (p)
1. Tibet (China)—Politics and government.
I. Ts'ao, ch'ang-ch'ing. II. Seymour, James D.
    DS786.T499    1997
    951'.505—dc21    97-26807
    CIP

Printed in the United States of America

The paper used in this publication meets the minimum requirements of American National Standard for Information Sciences— Permanence of Paper for Printed Library Materials, ANSI Z 39.48-1984.

BM (c)  10  9  8  7  6  5  4  3  2
BM (p)  10  9  8  7  6  5  4  3  2  1

# Contents

*Editors' Preface*     vii
*Introduction by James D. Seymour*     xi

Independence: The Tibetan People's Right
   *Cao Changching*     3
Brainwashing the Chinese
   *Cao Changching*     25
Tibetans' Rights and Chinese Intellectuals' Responsibility
   *Ding Zilin and Jiang Peikun*     31
Tibetan Chinese and Human Rights
   *Fang Lizhi*     37
Tibet: An Unavoidable Issue
   *Shen Tong*     41
Reflections on the Seventeen-point Agreement of 1951
   *Song Liming*     55
The Status of Tibet: Recalling a Visit to Lhasa
   *Wang Ruowang*     71
A Letter to Deng Xiaoping
   *Wei Jingsheng*     75
My View on the Tibet Issue
   *Harry Wu*     91
Independence and Unification
   *Xiang Xiaoji*     97

Ripple on the River of History
  *Xue Wei*   103

Federalism and the Future of Tibet
  *Yan Jiaqi*   107

Two Focuses of the Tibet Issue
  *Yiu Yung-chin*   121

*Contributors*   125
*Index*   129

# Editors' Preface

The purpose of this book is to convey to the international reader the thinking of one group of Chinese regarding the Tibet question. It is an outgrowth of a book that was published in Chinese in 1996;[1] however, we have not only translated but also expanded and reworked the book to make it accessible to the Western reader.

A word about style and semantics. Generally speaking, in translating and editing, we have taken the view that it is necessary to "let the Chinese be Chinese" and have resisted the temptation to make revisions just because it might make the text more suitable to Westerners. On the other hand, these writers often express themselves in ways that, if left unmediated, would tend to obscure rather than convey their meaning. For example, the Chinese have their own way of periodizing history: an era is defined by the term that each imperial house remained in power. Western historians tend to doubt that this gives an accurate picture of Chinese history, and it is definitely irrelevant to Tibetan history and to Sino-Tibetan relations. Thus in translation we often render "the such-and-such dynasty" in terms of the Western calendar.

Likewise, the Chinese have their own ideas of geography. "Tibet" is seen as roughly equivalent to today's truncated Tibet Autonomous Region (TAR). Because the Chinese authorities control mapmaking and because Western cartographers tend to take their cues from Beijing, the TAR is what shows up on most maps as "Tibet." But Tibetans have a different understanding.

For most, the TAR has no legitimacy, as it comprises only U and Tsang, areas traditionally administered locally by Lhasa and Shigatse, respectively; there is much more to Tibet than this. Ethnogeographically, it includes the entire Tibetan plateau. Amdo (what Chinese call Qinghai and Southern Gansu) and Kham (which includes what the Chinese consider Western Sichuan) and a small part of Yunnan are also ethnically Tibetan (even though the Lhasa government rarely controlled these areas). Even Chinese tend to consider this all one geographic entity ("the plateau"), referring to the other provinces as *neidi*, which literally means "interior," but actually refers to the Chinese heartland. Traditionally, *neidi* was the opposite of *bianwai*, or the lands outside China's national boundaries.

In this volume we will use the term *proper*, in the dictionary sense of "strictly limited to a specific ... place."[2] Thus "Tibet proper" denotes the TAR or some approximation thereof. The term *Inner Tibet*[3] denotes Amdo (Qinghai and South Gansu), eastern Kham (western Sichuan), and northern Yunnan. *Greater Tibet* denotes all of these together (Cholkha-sum). Use of the unmodified term *Tibet* will indicate that these distinctions were not considered significant for purposes of the immediate discussion. Finally, what in Chinese is called the *neidi* we shall call *China proper*.

Terms denoting ethnicity present a special difficulty. In English, it usually suffices simply to speak of *Chinese* and *Tibetans*. But the Chinese have a multiplicity of terms for "Chinese," the most common of which (*Zhongguo ren*) in the Chinese view includes Tibetans. When they mean to specify ethnic Chinese as distinct from "the minorities," they use the term *Han*. The writers in this book are in the habit of doing just this. But it often appears to be precisely a matter of habit rather than a political statement, and we believe that if they were speaking English they would not insist on this semantic distinction but would speak in the normal English way ("Chinese," "Tibetans"). Of course, when a writer like Wei Jingsheng intends to distinguish between "Chinese" and "Han," we keep the original vocabulary.

We are grateful to our translators Felicity Lung and Connie Cao. Others whose help we wish to acknowledge are Jigme Ngapo, Tseten Wangchuk, Jeanne Marie Gilbert, Linda McNell, Carol Schiller, and Tang Boqiao. Most especially we wish to acknowledge the untiring help of Connie Cao, who did the lion's share of editing and checking the translation. Without her help this book could not have appeared.

## Notes

1. Cao Changching, ed., *Zhongguo dalu zhishi fenzi lun Xizang* (Chinese mainland intellectuals on the subject of Tibet) (Taipei: Shidai Chuban Press, 1996).

2. *Webster's Ninth New Collegiate Dictionary*, p. 943.

3. The term *Inner Tibet* is not new with us, but we do not use it in precisely the traditional way.

# Introduction

## James D. Seymour

The Chinese learned about imperialism the hard way, having themselves been its victim for centuries. Unfortunately, many of the lessons they learned were the wrong ones. Even though the rest of the world has largely abandoned hegemonistic thinking, the Chinese have drawn the conclusion that a "modern" state must maximize its real estate and territorial waters.[1] Almost all Chinese cling to this idea and apply it to various territories and territorial waters to which China has some claim, legitimate or fancied. But in the case of Tibet, a magical, delicate country, though it had often fascinated the Chinese (as it does the rest of us) because of its beauty and spiritualism, only relatively recently has it become a target of Chinese imperialism. Before the present century, it was always others who invaded the country: the Mongols, Manchus, Dzungars, Nepalese, and British. Finally, in the twentieth century for the first time the Chinese (Hans) did so. Now, as so often happens with colonial powers, fascination for the "other" has given way to condescension and bigotry.

There are several different intellectual approaches to the problem of Tibet. Which approach one chooses largely determines how one will end up answering the question of whether Tibet legitimately (as Beijing says) "belongs to" China.[2] Almost all ethnic Chinese (whether communist or anticommunist) who think about the issue today have a set of facts, nonfacts, and principles that lead inevitably to the conclusion that Tibet is part of China's ancestral lands. Outside scholars who have studied the issue carefully in terms of international law find a few fragments of support for this claim, but probably a majority have concluded that China fails to meet the burden of proof. As for the Tibetans themselves, though they are not all of one mind, many conclude from their understanding of history that the Chinese simply have no business in Tibet.

In the present volume, we are exposed to yet a third perspective—that of some Chinese (most being exiles) who believe that Tibetans have been the victims of Chinese imperialism. Though this is the view of an infinitesimal minority of Chinese, history may still record the publication of the essays that follow as the first moment of a major turning point in history. After all, every decolonization movement in the world has involved not only a struggle for independence on the part of the subject people, but also support for them by a few gadflies among the colonizing race, perhaps radicals, perhaps moderates. In this collection, we hear from both. But even the relatively conservative of them, such as political scientist Yan Jiaqi, insist that the Tibetans are entitled at the very least to a high level of self-governance. For all the present so-called autonomous regions, Yan calls for the establishment of "autonomous states" that would exist within a Chinese federation and would have the power to enact their own basic laws. Thus, there would be some of the characteristics of a confederation. Furthermore, Yan would have each area enter into this order only with the approval of the various peoples, which in the case of Tibet might include Inner Tibet, that is, Qinghai Province and parts of Sichuan and Gansu provinces. Others among these writers go much further, arguing for outright independence. What is striking about all of them is that their frame of reference is Chinese, and yet they reach conclusions that seem very un-Chinese—if one is to accept the present hardline view as inherently "Chinese." They generally adhere to Chinese ways of conceptualizing the issue, but, armed with a knowledge of history and present-day Tibetan realities, they reach conclusions that are diametrically opposed to those of most of their compatriots. But is there anything inherently *Chinese* about the hardline view, or is it simply that irresponsible leaders, with a monopoly over the media, have been able to sell their own misguided version of social and historical realities?

At any rate, the purpose of this introduction is to contextualize this third set of views, and show how they relate to other approaches to the subject—Chinese, Tibetan, and international.

China's claim to Tibet typically rests on the following three contentions: First, it has insisted that Tibet has been part of China ever since what the Chinese call the Yuan dynasty (1280–1368). True, the empire has waxed and waned, but "waxing" is seen as normal, disunion and shrinkage abnormal. Second, all of the world's governments go along with, or at any rate do not seriously challenge, China's claim to sovereignty over Tibet. Finally, there is the indisputable fact that the Chinese Communists took over Tibet in the 1950s. They largely conquered Tibet in 1951 and by 1959 fully displaced the old regime there. Since then, the Chinese believe they have achieved legitimacy through quashing the old order of "feudal slavery" and instituting policies that are deemed beneficial (except during the admittedly counterproductive periods of "leftist" aberrations).

Chinese find it imperative that the empire's vicious cycles of florescence and decline be ended; and they believe this can only be effected through its transformation into a centralized, all-embracing state. Hardly any *Han* people in China question Beijing's position on such matters, for they have been exposed to no other nor to any reasonably objective account of the history of Sino-Tibetan relations. But, as Cao Changching observes below, in the absence of freedom of the press, all "information" is questionable, especially in the case of China, where "history" is controlled by media czars for whom truth is irrelevant. In fact, he notes, the China-based scholar Ya Hanzhang admitted in a treatise on Tibet's Dalai Lamas[3] that the book was written at the Communists' behest and pursuant to the Party's ideological line. So much for objectivity. Cao also points out that a translation of one of the leading Western works on the subject, by John F. Avedon,[4] was published in the People's Republic of China (PRC) but was then quickly banned with virtually all copies confiscated.

Thus it is not surprising that the Chinese have so much difficulty thinking clearly about the issue, much less relating to the Tibetans' views.

Another reason the Chinese have so much difficulty identifying with the Tibetans is that they project their own feelings of victimization onto them and assume that the Tibetans, being Chinese citizens, must feel the same way about it all. Thus, Tibetans had a brush with British imperialism; Chinese seem unaware that imperialists do not look so evil if they are a foil to *other* imperialists. The Chinese also argue that the Tibetans should not consider that their suffering at the hands of the Communists was anything special, for all Chinese suffered, especially during the Cultural Revolution. From the Tibetan point of view, what the Chinese did to themselves was their business; what they did to Tibet (bordering as it did on cultural genocide) had no parallel in China proper. The Chinese point out that many Tibetans participated in the "destroy the olds" campaign during which so many monasteries were destroyed. But Tibetans respond that these youngsters who were misled by the Maoists did not persist for long, whereas Cultural Revolution-type behavior by the Chinese has gone on much longer in Tibet than in China proper, where the phenomenon largely ended in the early 1970s. Thereafter, in incidents such as the Tiananmen demonstrations in 1989, Tibetans gave the Chinese people moral support; they wonder why such support has not been returned. The contributors to this volume have an answer. Cao, for example, has been influenced by Milan Kundura on the point that victims are not necessarily wiser than their oppressors. (He could as well have cited Paulo Friere.)[5] In Kundura's words, "The victims are no better than their oppressors. I can easily imagine their roles reversed."[6]

Thus, when Chinese citizens step outside their country, they are subjected to new information, ideas, and norms. Sometimes they are astonished at what they learn. Still, among exiles we find a broad spectrum of views regarding Tibet. This was already evidenced in October 1992, at a conference across the Potomac River from Washington, D.C. For two days, Tibetan and Chinese moderates (i.e., those seeking common ground, including several contributors to the present volume) met and considered the problem. Topics discussed included everything from the general problem of Sino-Tibetan relations to specialized topics pertaining to economics, politics, culture, and the environment. The papers and proceedings of the Potomac Conference are now computer-accessible to the public.[7]

The Chinese views expressed at the Potomac Conference ranged from shame at what had happened to Tibet, to noblesse oblige. A majority of the Chinese participants agreed with one another that although Chinese treatment of the Tibetans since 1950 had been morally indefensible, independence for Tibet would not be appropriate. Indeed, most Chinese intellectuals are infused with a sense of manifest destiny. When they point to historical support for this imperative, history is read selectively. Trivia is highlighted; essential facts are ignored. They point to the power of Chinese culture and civilization in assimilating various nationalities, such as inner Mongolia. They conveniently ignore the fact that most countries successfully resisted Chinese domination—including Vietnam, Korea, Japan, much of Mongolia, and (until the 1950s) Tibet.

Even overseas democratic activists, who can be learned and profound on most subjects, sometimes come across as ignorant and condescending when it comes to the subject of Tibet. Take, for example, Xu Bangtai, the respected editor of the journal *Zhongguo zhi chun* (China spring). At the Potomac Conference, Xu said that whereas Chinese nationalism (and even Taiwanese separatism) was rational, "the movement for the independence of Tibet is essentially emotional.... What I mean by an emotional movement is that the Tibet independence movement is driven by political and economic depression. The Tibetans demand a change of present conditions out of pain. The Tibetan independence movement does not have good political and economic foundations." Nor did it have much historical basis, he argued. He claimed (bogus) support for his argument from the Dalai Lama, who "did not deny that after the marriage of Song Zang

Gan Bu [Songtsen Gompo] and Princess Wen Chung in 821 A.D., the Tang dynasty and the Tu-bo [Tibet] kingdom signed a treaty to be 'one nation.' China has, for the most part, been administering Tibet ever since the Yuan dynasty was formed."[8]

To the Tibetans, such an attitude seems unhistorical, patronizing, and self-serving. To them, the quest for full sovereignty for their nation is as natural and rational as it was for the Chinese during their period of foreign incursions. Their historical starting point is not the Mongol period, which did not last very long and seems irrelevant. Rather, it is the seventh to ninth centuries, during which the Tibetans often bested the Tang China in battle.[9] In 821, after centuries of intermittent fighting, the two countries agreed on a treaty which many Tibetans like to believe stands as the definitive statement of proper Sino-Tibetan relations. The boundary was confirmed, and each country was to respect the territorial integrity of the other. China and Tibet were equals, and each promised mutual respect for the other's territorial sovereignty.

> Both Tibet and China shall keep their country and frontiers of which they are now in possession. The whole region to the east of that [frontier] being the country of Great China and the whole region to the west being the country of Great Tibet. From either side of that frontier there shall be no warfare, no hostile invasions, and no seizure of territory.[10]

The treaty detailed how diplomatic relations between the two countries were to be conducted, and these peaceful arrangements were to last for "ten thousand generations." Chinese are impressed by the fact that in this treaty the Tang *huangdi* and the Tibetan *tsanpo* (both terms meaning emperor) are referred to as *jiu* and *sheng*, which literally mean "uncle" and "nephew." However, Tibetans simply see these terms as referring to the fact that the young Tibetan ruler and the elderly Chinese emperor were distantly related.[11] In all material respects, in this treaty the two states are deemed equal. (The text of it is still enshrined on a stone monument in the center of Lhasa, now largely walled off from view.)

For all the importance Chinese like Xu Bangtai attach to the eighty-eight-year-long "Yuan dynasty," they consider irrelevant China's failure to continue the Mongols' mandate there during the long Ming period (1368–1644), inasmuch as "Chinese" influence was reasserted during the Qing (1644–1911). After that, the Kuomintang continued to insist that Tibet was part of their Republic, even though, like much of China, it was always beyond their effective control. At any rate, by mid-century Tibet was "liberated" by the Red Army (along with China proper, Inner Mongolia, and Eastern Turkestan), with Chinese sovereignty formalized in the 1951 Seventeen-point Agreement between the Beijing and Lhasa governments. All this is persuasive to almost all Chinese, both in China and abroad. The view is widely held that China has administered Tibet most of the time since the thirteenth century. In the present volume, on the other hand, democracy activist Wei Jingsheng, who at this writing is a political prisoner, denies that China had ever administered Tibet. That changed of course in the 1950s. But, as Cao Changching argues, the Seventeen-point Agreement that placed China in control is of questionable legality for various reasons. For the detached observer, the only immediately essential fact is that 1.2 billion Chinese share the orthodox view; they cannot hear from people like Wei and Cao.

It is not surprising that Tibetans perceive things differently, but it is novel to find the contributors to this volume expressing the views that they do. China's short-lived "Yuan dynasty" happened during a period when the Mongols ruled most of Asia, including China and Tibet; if this is to be the basis of China's claim to Tibet, Cao asks, why not claim *all* the former Mongol domains all the way across Asia to Eastern Europe? One might add that this factoid, if it had any significance at all, would give Mongolia as good a claim to Tibet as the Chinese. During the long Ming period of Chinese history, Tibet was entirely independent and was known in Chinese as Wu-si Zang or sometimes Wu-si Guo (*guo* meaning "country"). Scholars debate the question of how much influence the Manchus ("Qing") had over

Tibet after 1644. Few scholars would go as far as Cao does in claiming that their presence was only "nominal." At any rate, the Manchus were quite explicit that China and Outer Tibet were different countries. Outer Tibet (*Wai Zang*) was roughly the same as today's Tibet Autonomous Region. Tibetans are not so comfortable with the fact that Inner Tibet (*Nei Zang*, including Amdo/Qinghai and Kham/Xikang) was annexed to China.[12] But Outer Tibet, at least, was in the category *fan*, a somewhat ambiguous term that means "vassal" but is often interchanged or confused with another *fan*, which means "foreign" and with the similarly appearing *Tu*, short for Tubo, which was the way the Chinese then pronounced "Tibet." *Fan* countries included not only Tibet but also places as remote as Russia, where the Qing of course had no influence. Outer Tibet, to be sure, was a vassal. Still, the Manchu court did not consider it part of China. It was overseen by an "Imperial Resident Stationed in Tibet" (*Zhu Zang da chen*), who was answerable to the Fan-Managing Ministry (*Li fan yuan*), though on occasion he could memorialize the Manchu emperor directly. The Imperial resident was in charge of the Chinese soldiery and at least nominally of the Tibetan Army (*Tu bing*) as well.[13] (In his contribution to this book, Wei Jingsheng has an interesting interpretation of these matters.)

Neither the Mongols nor the Manchus were ethnic Chinese ("Hans"), and when each was expelled from authority their successors (Zhu Yuanzhang, Sun Yat-sen) had no interest in replacing them as overlords of Outer Tibet. Indeed, no ethnic Chinese government ever ruled Tibet until it was overrun in the 1950s by the Communists. Although the latter did force the Tibetans to accede to the Seventeen-point Agreement discussed below by Song Liming, this "agreement" strikes us as the ultimate in what the Chinese call "unequal treaties." Tibetans like Phuntsok Tashi Takla now deny the validity of this agreement because of the manner in which it was imposed, because the Chinese themselves violated its terms, and for certain technical reasons having to do with how the document was drawn up.

So on the first point (the Chinese claim that Tibet was part of

China since the Yuan dynasty), the Tibetans would seem to have the better of the argument.

The Chinese do somewhat better on the second point. One generally understood condition of sovereignty is that the international community acknowledge such sovereignty. The community of states has indeed recognized China's claim to Tibet. Tibetans do have their champions, for example the U.S. Congress (which has passed resolutions affirming Tibet as an occupied country), and also in formerly occupied countries like Lithuania. In Buddhist Japan, the idea of establishing formal ties with the Dalai Lama is popular,[14] though the government is unlikely to make any moves in that direction. In the case of the executive branch of the American government, the position has not been altogether consistent. In recent years, the State Department position has been the following: "The United States ... considers Tibet to be a part of China, with the status of an autonomous region.... The United States has never taken the position that Tibet is an independent country.... We are for the self-determination of Tibet, but self-determination is not necessarily equated with independence."[15] True enough, but if independence is disallowed as an option, meaningful self-determination cannot take place. Thus Congress has continued to press in various ways, such as passing a law that Tibet must be dealt with separately from China in the State Department's Human Rights Report.[16]

However, if the other requirements of sovereignty are met, international recognition of China's claim would seem to be insufficient legal grounds to deny Tibet its sovereignty. To reason otherwise would have the international community arguing, in effect: Although you may meet the requirements of sovereignty, you lack that right because we choose to deny it. Actually the international-recognition requirement only makes sense if one views the nations as a jury that decides whether a nation qualifies for sovereignty; it does not give the international community the right to disregard the objective circumstances.

The Chinese authorities are on their weakest legal and moral ground when it comes to their third argument. Conquest, in this day and age, is by definition illegitimate. As Wei Jingsheng puts it: "The will and aspiration of the people are the main constituting factor of sovereignty. . . . Military occupation and administrative control cannot change this principle, especially in modern times."

As for proving their virtue through beneficent rule, the writers of this volume make it clear that it has not been so beneficent. Wei is withering on this point. The participants of the Potomac Conference—both Chinese and Tibetan—were basically in agreement. Phintso Thonden may have been indulging in a bit of hyperbole when, in his address there, he asserted that China had made "billions of dollars" in Tibet "in the earlier years of its occupation," leaving the country "an empty shell of its former self," and he did acknowledge that today China spends more there than it derives. But he and many other participants of both nationalities saw these expenditures as being of little benefit to the Tibetan people, and they roundly condemned recent policies which have resulted in ecological deterioration. Some have been less quick to condemn the Chinese, in the belief that they have made some contributions to Tibet and that the traditional Tibetan order was not without its drawbacks. But there was general agreement that the Chinese occupation has been no boon to the Tibetan people.

Even were Tibet prospering, Tibetans correctly view economics as irrelevant to the sovereignty issue, especially in view of the increasingly integrated international economy. In both of the international human rights covenants,[17] the very first articles identically assert: "All peoples have the right to self-determination. By virtue of that right they freely determine their political status and freely pursue their economic, social, and cultural development."[18] Beijing has sometimes been at the forefront of the efforts to implement this provision in other parts of the world but has denied its applicability to the British colony of Hong Kong, to the former Japanese colony of Taiwan, and to the nonethnic Chinese parts of the PRC. By and large the governments of the world have gone along with China on this.

Still, the cause of Tibetan independence has received increasing international attention in recent years. And even those who deny that Tibet is entitled to independence have to accept the fact that Tibetans at least comprise an *indigenous group* within the meaning of the term as used in international law. According to the most widely accepted definition, indigenous peoples are "descendants of the original inhabitants of conquered territories possessing a minority culture and recognizing themselves as such."[19] In legal parlance, such peoples comprise "nonstate nations." Thus, under the principle of "prior sovereignty" (under the Tang, Ming, and perhaps Republic) Tibet would at least have the right to autonomy. Of course this is still an emerging area of international law, but the general concept seems to have been accepted *in principle* even by China, when it designates "minority" areas as "autonomous regions" and "autonomous districts." However, China has not accepted this *in practice*, for in reality these regions have no autonomy; they are ruled by central government appointees in general disregard of the will and rights of the indigenous population.

Human rights problems in Tibet have been receiving increasing attention and have even come before the United Nations Human Rights Commission in Geneva. Prodded by Tibetan exiles and also by nongovernmental organizations,[20] certain countries (and particularly the European Union) have provided strong resolutions sharply critical of China's record there. One such resolution in 1992 was successfully opposed by the United States and China (with its Third World supporters), because it was less than clear on the sovereignty question. Their opposing view, that the integrity of the state took precedence over the rights of national self-determination, prevailed. In spite of such occasional American support for its point of view, China complains that Western concern for Tibetans' human rights is a cover for imperialistic designs.[21] Whether or not this view is misguided, it is understandable given Britain's historic meddling in Tibet and CIA assistance to Tibetan guerrillas in the 1950s and 1960s.[22] Thus the Chinese have so far been successful in sidetracking UN efforts to examine human abuses in Tibet.

Thus when we Westerners (and Japanese) get involved in the Tibet issue, the Chinese reaction is apt to be highly charged. Many people are quick to scent a resurgence of foreign imperialism. Even many Hong Kong people are vehemently opposed to independence for Tibet. For example, one writer has maintained that "foreigners ... have no business supporting [Tibetans'] *political* goal of independence.... I think some of [these foreigners who do so] are simply anti-China racists."[23] Actually, while the writer's general point that people should not interfere in the internal political affairs of other countries is well taken, on this issue the international human rights covenants (quoted above) mandate to the contrary: "The States Parties to the present Covenant ... shall promote the realization of the right of self-determination."

Chinese claims do not rest merely on history and international law; there is also perceived national necessity. They have come up with a long list of reasons why China *must* possess Tibet. China needs the space and the region's economic resources. Then there is the matter of security and the memory of the 1962 war with India. Thus even the more enlightened Chinese tend to think of the Tibet question in terms of economic, political, and military imperatives, rather than what is just and legal.[24] The Chinese have their own peculiar version of the "domino theory." They worry that Tibetan independence would be followed by Xinjiang, Inner Mongolia, and Manchuria going their own ways (even though in none of these is there a single non-Han race in the majority). China's leaders are sufficiently concerned to put such considerations ahead of all others. In Deng Xiaoping's words, China must retain Tibet whether doing so is "right or wrong."[25]

Tibetans have a mirror image of such considerations. For them, there has been the trauma of being overrun by China in the 1950s, of the exodus, and of having the homeland's cultural institutions destroyed during the following decades. Had China pursued more humane policies toward Tibet, it is conceivable they would now be in a position to persuade the people there that their best future lay in throwing in their lot with China. But as it is, many Tibetans refuse to consider any future for Tibet other than total independence from China. Furthermore, they consider it a matter of urgency, lest their country be overrun by Han immigrants, as happened in Inner Mongolia and Manchuria, and may be happening in what the Chinese call their "New Territories" (*Xinjiang*) and some others call "Eastern Turkestan." However, in the case of outer Tibet, such fears may be overdrawn, for Chinese usually find Tibet culturally and ecologically inhospitable, and those who go there do not generally deem it to be their permanent residences.

Opinions about Tibet vary widely within both the Chinese and Tibetan communities. There are extremists and moderates on both sides. At the Potomac Conference, the moderates were represented. In this book we hear from people who, were they Tibetans, would be considered moderate, though most Chinese doubtless consider their views extreme and will be shocked that fellow Chinese could express such "splittist" views. But these writers believe that one can be a good Chinese without being imperialistic. They remember that China's real cultural achievements historically had little to do with militarism and imperialism and that Chinese civilization reached its qualitative peaks during the relatively peaceful and culture-oriented (albeit small) Song and Ming Chinas. To people of this persuasion, these dynasties, unencumbered as they were by the martial spirit of the Mongols, Manchus, and Communists, represented the real China. While these views may not be well received today, history has a way of vindicating "extremists" when reason and justice are on their side.

But that is not going to happen soon. Not only do conservative Chinese cling to anachronistic imperialistic notions, but even the democracy movement is comprised largely of self-styled patriots who have no desire to see the diminution of the territory of the PRC. Already it is clear that this issue is one of the democracy movement's major challenges.[26] Even these Democrats sometimes subscribe to the most extreme version of the domino theory—that once Tibet goes, all the other provinces will fall like dominoes and the former China will become thirty independent countries.[27] Nevertheless, most of the contributors to the present volume once accepted Chinese orthodoxy on the Tibet question; as they were exposed to an undistorted version of history, and international concepts of sovereignty and nationality rights, their thinking changed, though not their "Chineseness." Many others will likely experience the same growth.

Although all the writers who have contributed to this volume accept the principle of self-determination, the degree of their enthusiasm for independence varies. Some, including Cao Changching, accept it as natural, logical, and inevitable. Others, like Wei Jingsheng, consider that independence would be the least desirable outcome, a product of the blundering of China's leaders, whom he so scorns. Although they would leave the choice up to the Tibetans, they would be saddened if the Tibetans make the wrong choice. Some seem to harbor the hope that, even if the Tibetans gained their independence, there is hope that they would eventually see the light and reassociate with China. Although this seems unlikely, there is some international precedent: in 1996 Russia and Belarus' took the initial steps to form a "Community of Sovereign Republics." Viewed in the context of East Asian history, that would be a very Chinese solution, and might not be a bad outcome for Tibet.

It may seem odd to insist that these writers are expressing very *Chinese* points of view, and most Chinese would surely disagree. But after all, no ethnic Chinese emperor in history ever considered Tibet as part of China. That traditional understanding persisted into the twentieth century, now influenced by Wilsonian idealism. Sun Yat-sen insisted on the right of self-determination for such peoples as the Tibetans, and the 1923 Sun-Joffe Manifesto called for autonomy for them. The next year the principles of autonomy and self-determination were incorporated into the Guomindang's official platform; racial minorities who so desired were to enjoy self-determination and self-government. In the 1930s the Communists likewise insisted on this principle. The constitution of the Jiangxi Soviet declared:

> The Soviet government of China has recognized the right of self-determination of the national minorities in China, their right to *complete separation* from China, and to the formation of an independent state for each national minority. All Mongolians, Tibetans, Miao, Yao, Koreans, and others living on the territory of China shall enjoy the full right of self-determination, i.e., they may either join the Union of Chinese Soviets or secede from it and form their own state as they may prefer. [Emphasis added.][28]

Mao Zedong more or less held to this view until after World War II. In 1936 he told Edgar Snow that Korea, Taiwan, and the Moslem minorities could have independence. Because Inner Mongolia had so many Chinese, it could only be an "autonomous state." Soon he modified his position somewhat: Areas without large Chinese populations, such as Tibet, would form "autonomous republics attached to the China federation."[29] The first ethnic Chinese ruler in history to insist that Tibet must belong to China was Chiang Kai-shek, whom very few today look upon as a hero.

The "Chineseness" of the protagonists represented in this volume is both a strength and a weakness. Above, reference has been made to international trends and international standards regarding such issues as sovereignty, "prior sovereignty," decolonization, and the rights of indigenous groups. These are all international legal concepts with which Chinese on all sides of the argument indicate little resonance or even familiarity. Perhaps, as their thinking evolves, they will be more influenced by such considerations. But intellectual evolution will not necessarily be in one direction. Mao Zedong's thinking went from favoring self-determination (permitting independence) to insisting on unification. If and when the more liberal Chinese Democrats come to power, it is possible they, too, would lose their enthusiasm for self-determination for Tibet.[30]

But not necessarily. Things would be different then, for China would have a free press and the public would not be kept in captive ignorance. The costs of empire, both financial and moral, would become increasingly obvious and unacceptable. This situation would be like France in the mid-1950s during the final effort to retain Algeria as "an integral part of metropolitan France." Whatever the context it will not be pleasant, but there is a chance that the end result will be just. And, as Cao notes, justice is essential if genuine democracy is to come to China. This means, first and foremost, a just resolution of China's various ethnic problems.

## Notes

1. As the Mongolian scholar U.E. Bulag has commented to me: "The issue of Tibet in China is not just an internal problem, but it is a contesting platform against the Western invasion that humiliated the Chinese for many decades."
2. See Beijing's White Paper: "Tibet—Its Ownership and Human Rights Situation," *Beijing Review*, September 28, 1992, pp. 10–43.
3. *Dalai Lama Zhuan* (Beijing: Renmin chuban she, 1963), p. 1.
4. Originally published as *In Exile from the Land of the Snows* (London: Michael Joseph, 1984). A copy of the Chinese text was smuggled into India and eventually republished in Taiwan as *Xueyu jingwai liu wangji* (Taipei: Caituan Faren Press, 1991).
5. *Pedagogy of the Oppressed* (New York: Continuum, 1983).
6. Milan Kundura, *The Farewell Party* (New York: Penguin, 1977), p. 70.
7. The gopher address is: "gopher://gopher.cc.columbia.edu:71/11/clioplus/scholarly/South Asia/Tibet." Subcategory: "Potomac Conference 1992." Also available via Telnet and WWW.
8. See gopher site in note 7. In 1996, Xu repeated these views (and made a gratuitous personal attack on me) in "Sima Jin zhi xin, wuren dang zhi" (We know Seymour's heart), *Zhongguo zhi chun*, August 1966, pp. 90–95, and editorial, pp. 3–4.
9. The Chinese have also been known to cite the Tang period as the starting point of Sino-Tibetan relations, but this was so counterproductive in terms of advancing their cause that they have largely dropped the era from official accounts of Sino-Tibetan relations. Still, the idea is not completely dead. See, for example, Xinhua dispatch of September 26, 1992 (English translation in U.S. Joint Publications Research Service, CAR-92–007, October 13, 1992, pp. 34–35), in which it is stated that the fact that a Tang official traveling to India went via Tibet "proved that the country was already an important official channel of the Tang dynasty."
10. Michael C. Walt van Praag, *The Status of Tibet: History, Rights, and Prospects in International Law* (Boulder, Colo.: Westview, 1987), appendix.

11. One of the Tsanpo's stepmothers was a niece of Tang dynasty founder Taizong, who was an ancestor of Gao Zong, the Chinese emperor who signed the treaty as "uncle."

12. The terms *Nei Zang* and *Hou Zang* are not to be confused with *Qian Zang* (the area under the control of Lhasa) and *Hou Zang* (the area under the control of Shigatse).

13. The Qing administration in Tibet is described in H. S. Brunnert and V. V. Hagelstrom, *Present Day Political Organization of China* (Shanghai: Kelly and Walsh, 1912), pp. 465–77.

14. The Hong-Kong based *Far Eastern Economic Review*, August 8, 1996, p. 29, conducted a survey of its readers in ten countries and found that 52.6 of the Japanese favored such ties. Overall, only 33 percent of readers agreed; 67 percent answered in the negative.

15. Testimony by L. Desaix Anderson, Principal Deputy Assistant Secretary of State, before the Senate Foreign Relations Committee, on July 28, 1992. (The last sentence was in response to a question.)

16. This the State Department has done grudgingly. The report on Tibet issued in 1995 begins with the parenthetical comment: "(This section of the report on China has been prepared pursuant to section 536 (b) of Public Law 103–236. The United States [meaning the executive branch] recognizes the Tibet Autonomous Region (hereinafter referred to as 'Tibet') to be part of the People's Republic of China. Preservation and development of Tibet's unique religious, cultural, and linguistic heritage and protection of its people's fundamental human rights continue to be of concern.)"

17. In 1966 the United Nations (with the PRC then still excluded) adopted two detailed covenants on human rights: the International Covenant on Civil and Political Rights and the International Covenant on Economic, Social, and Cultural Rights. By 1976 both covenants had been accepted by enough countries to be considered "in force" at least with respect to the ratifying countries. Though their applicability to nonsignatories like China is a moot point of international law, the illegitimacy of colonialism is not subject to dispute.

18. What the international human rights covenants seem to say is that a "people" of a disputed territory with a plausible argument for sovereignty should decide for themselves whether they are to be an independent country or annexed to another country. Although it is not made clear what is a "people," in 1961 the UN General Assembly declared that the Tibetans met all the requirements for self-determination.

19. Jeff J. Corntassal and Thomas Hopkins Primeau, "Indigenous 'Sovereignty' and International Law: Revised Strategies for Pursuing 'Self-Determination,'" *Human Rights Quarterly* 12:2 (May 1995): 346. My discussion of indigenous groups draws on this article.

20. Most visible are such general human rights organizations as Amnesty International and Human Rights Watch. Especially effective and reliable on Tibetan issues is Tibet Information Network (London).

21. See Sun Zhengda, *Xizang wenti yu Meiguo de "renquan waijiao"*

[American "human rights diplomacy" and the problem of Tibet], in *Waiguo wenti yanjiu* [Studies in foreign affairs], special issue on human rights, no. 2 (March 15, 1990): 76–81.

22. On the CIA's activities, see A. Tom Grunfeld, *The Making of Modern Tibet* (Armonk, N.Y.: M. E. Sharpe, 1987; rev. ed., 1996), especially pp. 149–53. Regarding Britain's role, PRC delegate Zhang Yishan declared to the UN's Third Committee that there are no human rights problems in Tibet, and added: "I'd like to tell the British delegate: Those things that could not be achieved in colonial times can never be achieved today" (NCNA, November 25, 1992, Foreign Broadcast Information Service [FBIS], November 25, 1992, p. 1).

23. Wing C. Ng, "Tibet," *AHKCUS Quarterly*, no. 13 (May 1994): 11. Another article in the same issue was more open-minded: Andrew Au, "On Tibet and a Greater China," pp. 12–13.

24. See Au, "On Tibet and a Greater China."

25. Quoted by Cao Changching, below.

26. The very mention of Tibet's right to self-determination has already caused some erstwhile members of the Chinese Alliance for Democracy to threaten to leave the movement and support the communists as the only way to prevent the disintegration of "China."

27. See, for example, a letter from CAD member in South Africa about how area supporters are leaving the movement. *Beijing zhi chun*, April 1995, p. 104.

28. Constitution of the Soviet Republic (1931), in Conrad Brandt, Benjamin Schwartz, and John K. Fairbank, *A Documentary History of Chinese Communism*, (New York: Atheneum, 1966), p. 223.

29. Edgar Snow, *Red Star over China* (New York: Grove, 1961), part 3, sec. 3, p. 96.

30. Yan Jiaqi, one of the contributors to this volume, remarked on the occasion of the Potomac Conference: "China will not tolerate losing its geopolitical screen. . . . No Chinese government will allow that to happen." See note 7 for Potomac Conference site.

# TIBET
Through
Dissident
Chinese Eyes

# Independence:
# The Tibetan People's Right

## Cao Changching

The Chinese governments on both sides of the Taiwan Strait hold opposing views on most issues, often resorting to verbal attacks and tit-for-tat maneuverings. On the Tibet issue, however, the two sides cling to the same notion: both claim Chinese sovereignty over Tibet and claim that the territory has been a part of China since ancient times. Through a brief review of Chinese history, however, we can clearly see that Tibet had never been a part of China until it was invaded and occupied by the Chinese in the 1950s.

**The Historic Relationship between Tibet and China**

China proper was unified in 221 B.C. Less than a century later, in 127 B.C., the first Tibetan king was crowned. For the next few centuries tribal civil wars plagued Tibet. In the seventh century A.D., about the period of China's Tang dynasty, King Songsten Gampo of Tibet conquered the various tribes, unified Tibet, and expanded its territory. The country became very powerful during this period. The Tibetan army was strong enough to conquer China's capital, Chang'an (now Xi'an). Princess Wen Cheng of the Tang dynasty was given in marriage to King Songsten Gampo—a political maneuver designed to facilitate relations between Tibet and China.

At the end of China's Song dynasty (1279), both Tibet and China were conquered by the Mongol leader Genghis Khan, whose cavalry actually occupied most of Asia. The Mongols established a capital on Chinese territory to rule over some of the conquered lands. The Chinese know this as the Yuan period. As a Buddhist, the emperor Kublai Khan recognized the authority of Grand Lama Phagpa, Tibet's highest lama, to act as the leading lama for the Yuan dynasty. He was something like a *guoshi* [literally, "national instructor"]. But within Tibet the emperor also gave him political power in addition to his religious role. Therefore the Mongols did not rule Tibet directly.

When the Mongol Empire fell, it was replaced in China by the Ming dynasty, during which period Tibet and China had virtually no contact. Thus China's claim to sovereignty over Tibet depends largely on its relationship with Tibet during the subsequent period of Manchu rule, known to Chinese as the Qing dynasty (1644–1911). Thus much of the discussion below concerns Sino-Tibetan relations under the Manchus.

China's relationship with Tibet during the Qing dynasty was essentially amicable. On four occasions, at the request of the Dalai Lama, the Qing army marched into Tibet to assist the Tibetans in defending against foreign invasions and in repressing rebellions. Each time, after the disputes were settled, the Qing army was immediately recalled back to China. At the end of the Qing dynasty, Tibet was invaded by Nepal and England. In 1909, after the death of the Guangxu emperor and the empress dowager, Ci Xi, the Qing army stormed into Tibet and occupied it. Two years later, in 1911, the Chinese democratic revolution led by Sun Yat-sen overthrew the Qing dynasty and established the Republic. The old Qing army stationed in Tibet split into two warring factions. One faction supported the emperor, the other favored the Republic. Taking advantage of turmoil within the Qing army, the Tibetans organized an uprising and ultimately gained power over the local Qing forces; the Thirteenth Dalai Lama then announced Tibet's independence.

During the forty years from the 1911 Revolution through 1950 Tibet was essentially an independent country. Following the death of the Thirteenth Dalai Lama in 1933 and the selection of the present Fourteenth Dalai Lama it underwent a transition. The Chinese government made a great effort to incorporate Tibet into China, and President Chiang Kai-shek twice sent his special envoys to Lhasa to try to persuade the Tibetans to become subjects of the Republic. The Tibetan leaders, however, never consented to this. A collection of hundreds of documents recently compiled in China, containing nearly five hundred communications between Chiang's government and its representatives in Lhasa, clearly demonstrates that Tibet never agreed to be under China's control during the Republican period.[1]

In early 1950, immediately after the establishment of the People's Republic of China (PRC), the Chinese Communist army made preparations to conquer Tibet. While a large Chinese military force was bearing down on the Tibetan border, the Tibetans sent a delegation to Beijing in an attempt to secure peace. As is described elsewhere in this volume, however, the delegation was finally obliged to sign the Seventeen-point Agreement.

## Positions of the Two Chinese Governments

The Chinese government's claim to sovereignty over Tibet depends largely on six points:

1. During the Tang period (618–907), the Tibetan king Songsten Gampo married Princess Wen Cheng. The princess is said to have wielded tremendous influence over Tibet.

2. During the Yuan dynasty (1271–1368), Tibet was part of the Mongol Empire and under Yuan rule.

3. During the period of Manchu rule (1644–1911), the Qing army entered Tibet to protect it on several occasions.

4. The title of "Dalai Lama" was created by the Qing emperor and was first bestowed on the Fifth Dalai Lama.

5. During the control of Chiang Kai-shek's Republican gov-

ernment, Wu Zhongxin, chair of the Committee on Mongolia and Tibet, was sent to Lhasa to confirm the reincarnation and to host the inauguration of the fourteenth Dalai Lama.

6. Tibet had no formal diplomatic relations with any other countries.[2]

All this has been misinterpreted, however, and does not support the conclusions the Chinese are trying to draw.

1. The marriage of Tang dynasty Princess Wen Cheng and King Songsten Gampo was a strategic effort to secure peace and cooperation between the two countries. It is absurd to base China's claim to sovereignty over Tibet on the fact of this marriage.

2. Genghis Khan, the Mongol conqueror, occupied most of Eurasia, including China, Tibet, Vietnam, and Korea. The Yuan period is referred to as a Chinese dynasty because the Mongols established a capital on the territory belonging to the Chinese (Han) people, from which it ruled over conquered lands. China argues that Tibet is a part of Chinese territory because Tibet was also conquered by the Mongol empire at this time. If military occupation qualifies as a historical claim to ownership, it would best be made by the Mongols, not the Chinese. Furthermore, if the fact that Tibet was once ruled by the Yuan dynasty forms a legal basis for the Chinese to claim sovereignty over Tibet, why have the Chinese never made the same claim to Vietnam, Korea, and other parts of Asia that were annexed and ruled over by the Mongols at the same time?

3. True, the Qing army, at the request of Tibetan authorities, was sent to Tibet four times to help settle internal rebellions and to defeat external invasions. This alone, however, does not support the Chinese claim to ownership of Tibet. If it did, the United States would have gained sovereign rights to Kuwait after its intervention in defense of Kuwait against Iraq. Similarly, the United States could claim rights over Haiti because it assisted Haiti in restoring democracy.

4. It is historically inaccurate to say that the title of Dalai Lama was created by the Qing emperor. This point is even acknowledged in the book *Biographies of the Dalai Lamas,* by Ya

Hanzhang, a leading Beijing scholar on Tibet. Ya admits that the title of Dalai Lama was not created by the Qing emperor, but in fact had been first bestowed upon Sonam Gyatso, a religious leader of Tibet, by the Mongol ruler Altan Khan, during the time corresponding to the Chinese Ming dynasty.[3] Actually *Dalai* is Mongolian for "sea." *Lama* is Tibetan for "wise master." The Tibetan religious leaders prior to Sonam Gyatso were identified posthumously as the First and Second Dalai Lama. Sonam Gyatso is identified as the Third Dalai Lama. From then on, the title of Dalai Lama has been used.

It is true that a Qing emperor once conferred on the fifth Dalai Lama a twenty-four-word title, which included the words "Dalai Lama." But in those days the Dalai Lama also gave the emperor many titles.[4] This custom of giving titles was a gesture of good will and is not evidence of any subordination.

5. Both the Communists and Nationalists claim that a representative from Chiang Kai-shek's government, Wu Zhongxin, was sent to Lhasa to confirm the reincarnation and to preside over the Fourteenth Dalai Lama's enthronement ceremony in 1939. They treat this as proof that Tibet is a part of China. However, the telegrams between Wu and the Chiang government[5] clearly indicate that Tibet was merely making a face-saving gesture for Chiang's government by permitting Wu to attend the reincarnation and to participate in the ceremony. Wu had no power in the choosing of the Fourteenth Dalai Lama. Similarly Ya Hanzhang wrote in his book, *Biographies of the Dalai Lamas,* that "The so-called observation was merely to enable Chiang's government to save face. In reality, there was no veto power."[6] An argument arose during the enthronement ceremony when Wu was given an ordinary seat. The issue was resolved when the Tibetans finally agreed to seat Wu in the area normally reserved for foreign ambassadors. Ya wrote, "About the seating issue, it was merely to regain face for Chiang's government. This was to show that Wu's position was at least on a par with that of ambassadors."[7]

Although Wu did not host the enthronement, the Guomindang

newspaper printed a photograph of the Dalai Lama with Wu as evidence that Wu had hosted the ceremony. However, in a speech by Ngapo Ngawang Jigme, former vice chairman of the Chinese National People's Congress, published in *Tibet Daily* in 1989, it was stated that the photograph had been taken when Wu went to pay a visit to the Dalai Lama in his bedroom, not at the enthronement ceremony at all.[8] Furthermore, two of the communications between Lhasa and Chongqing during this period clearly demonstrate Wu's secondary role. The first, "official letter No. 439," was a telegram from Dong Xianguang, the deputy minister of Chiang's Propaganda Department, to Wu Zhongxin in Lhasa, informing Wu that the Associated Press wanted a photograph of the Dalai Lama at the ceremony.[9] Wu replied with the second document, a telegram saying that because the ceremony had taken place in the morning, it had not been possible to take pictures. Instead, he responded that he would send pictures of other events.[10] It is difficult to believe that if Wu had been host, there would have been no pictures of the ceremony.

6. That Tibet had no formal diplomatic relations with other countries and depended on the Qing army to secure its peace was because Tibet was a theocracy. Tibet and China had a close relationship mainly during the Qing dynasty. The dynamics of this relationship was based on a "patron–priest" relationship. The Qing emperor was the patron. He gave military assistance as well as money and gifts to the Dalai Lama. This helped the Dalai Lama not only to assert political and religious power in Tibet but to become the highest religious leader of the Qing empire. In return, the Dalai Lama helped the Qing dynasty to maintain stability by using his religious influence in many countries, such as Mongolia, Korea, Vietnam, and Burma. Tibet and China had a cooperative, mutually beneficial relationship. This relationship was similar to the relationship between Italy and the Vatican. Although the Vatican happens to be located on the Italian peninsula, it is not a province of Italy; in fact it does not belong to Italy at all. If the Vatican were attacked and the Swiss Guards could not handle the situation, the pope would presumably request that

the Italian police or army come to its assistance. But the Vatican would not come under Italy's sovereignty as a result of any such military intervention.

One might also say that relations between Tibet and China were analogous to the relationship between an East Asian village and a temple on a nearby mountain. The head of this village and many villagers are Buddhists, they look to the lama at the temple as a spiritual leader. The head of the village does not have power to handle temple matters. But if robbers invade the temple, or if the young monks rebel, the village head would respond to the lama's requests for help and would send his gendarmes to the temple. Then, after order has been restored, the gendarmes would leave the temple. In normal times, as a patron, the village provides food to the temple. The temple does not maintain its own armed forces, because Buddhism advocates nonviolence. In emergencies, the temple can ask the village head to send armies for protection. For the village head, it is good politics to oblige. He gains support from his Buddhist villagers by showing respect and support for the lama. The temple does not need to declare independence as it has never belonged to the village. The relationship between the lama and the village head is to the advantage of all. Any severing of the relationship would be initiated by the village head, not by the lama. This could happen if, for example, the temple were in trouble and the village head refused to help or actually intended to take over the temple. The temple survives on spiritual power, not by the service of an army. If the village head does not believe in religion and wants to occupy the temple forcibly or even to transform the Buddhists socially, then the temple would have no alternative but to wave a white flag and surrender.

Thus, because of the special nature of Tibet as a theocracy and its patron–priest relations with China, it was an independent country in a unique way, for it did not establish formal diplomatic relations with other nations. But such relations are a trivial issue. It often happens that two nations do not have diplomatic relations. Sometimes its absence has to do with questions of territorial sovereignty, but usually it does not. For example, the United States does not have diplomatic relations with Cuba, but that does not affect Cuba's right to have its own nation-state. Therefore we cannot say that because Tibet did not have formal diplomatic relations with other countries, it thereby lost its national sovereignty.

Other examples show that Tibet was not subordinate to China. In 1652, the Qing Shunzhi emperor invited the Fifth Dalai Lama for a friendly visit to China. According to Ya, in preparation for the Dalai Lama's visit to Beijing, the Qing emperor discussed with his ministers the formalities of welcoming the Dalai Lama. The Manchu ministers urged the emperor to welcome the Dalai Lama personally in the outskirts of the city because the Dalai Lama was a state master. It was thought that this gesture would ensure the allegiance of Mongolia, which was predominately Buddhist. But the Han ministers believed that the "emperor is the leader of all countries" and to go out of the city to welcome the Dalai Lama personally would be beneath the emperor's dignity. Finally the Shunzhi emperor came up with a solution. He went out of town conducting what was billed as a hunting expedition and just "happened" to encounter the Fifth Dalai Lama.[11]

Actually, in all of Chinese history no emperor ever left the city to welcome a person under his authority. Even during the end of the Qing dynasty, in the face of visits by envoys from the-then powerful England, the emperor insisted that the envoys worship the emperor by kneeling. Also in Ya's book, there are prints of two mural paintings depicting the Shunzhi Emperor with the Fifth Dalai Lama, and the Empress Dowager Ci Xi with the Thirteenth Dalai Lama, each pair sitting side by side. Far from being treated as a subordinate, the Dalai Lamas received these special courtesies.

Had Tibet been subordinate to the Qing dynasty it would have been incumbent, like other provinces and affiliated countries under the Qing rule, to pay tribute to the emperor. History does not record such a relationship. On the contrary, Qing officials frequently presented gifts to Tibet because the Qing government respected the Dalai Lama as a spiritual leader and acknowledged Buddhism as the state religion. This friendly relationship lasted almost 260 years—through the entire period of the Qing dynasty.

Thus, with the minor exception that Tibet did not have formal relations with other nations, it has had all the normal characteristics of a sovereign nation-state. For example, Tibet has had (1) its own culture, language, and customs; (2) an established method of selecting its head of state (the Dalai Lama); (3) its own government (though it is now in exile); (4) its own capital, Lhasa; (5) its own laws enacted by the Tibetans themselves; (6) its own tax system, printing and issuing its own currency, as well as administering its own finances; (7) its own army; (8) natural [geographic] borders between Tibet and other countries, including China; and (9) its own unique and discrete history.

**Tibet Today**

Though both have had much to say on the subject, neither the authorities in Taiwan nor those in the People's Republic of China appear to understand the history of Tibet. Most Chinese people's knowledge of Tibetan history is heavily influenced by their respective governments. Because the two Chinese governments consistently claim that Tibet is part of China's territory, books on the history of Tibet as the independent country that it was are rarely published in either place. Indeed, the Chinese version of this volume, which has been published in Taiwan, was the first such work. What most Chinese have read about Tibet is quite different from that.

In October 1992 the People's Republic of China published "Tibet: Its Ownership and Human Rights Situation," the so-called *White Paper* on Tibet. This report followed the dictate of Deng Xiaoping, who had said that "essentially Tibet is part of China. This is the criterion for judging right or wrong."[12] These words are outrageous. Alas, Deng's words expressed the thoughts of many Chinese. People have maintained this belief despite a lack of understanding of Tibet's history, a lack of research on Tibet's current condition, and a lack of knowledge of Tibetan and Western scholars' research. Instead, the Chinese have held to their beliefs and have blocked out the Tibetans' voices.

Although respect for history is a basic starting point in discussing the Tibet issue, more important is that we understand the Tibetan people's current plight and respect their wishes. We can judge the current Tibet condition by asking the following questions: Do the Tibetans enjoy basic political rights? Is their right to private property protected? Are they becoming more prosperous, or are they instead suffering from poverty? Is religious freedom respected, or is it trampled on? Is Tibet's culture and natural environment protected or have they been damaged? Do Chinese treat Tibetans with respect or do they discriminate against them?

A mere glimpse of Tibet's current situation will reveal the atrocities that have taken place. The Tibetans are completely deprived of their right to vote, as is the case with all Chinese. There is not one level of government that represents the will of the people. The general secretary of the regional Communist Party committee holds the highest power in Tibet. From the 1959 "suppression of the rebellion" to the present, none of the seven secretaries of this committee has been Tibetan.

Tibet, like the rest of the PRC, does not have political freedom. The Chinese military represses any form of opposition. According to reports from the Chinese army stationed in Tibet, eighty-seven thousand Tibetans were killed in the suppression of the 1959 rebellion.[13] According to the figures of the late Tenth Panchen Lama, who was once the vice chairman of the Chinese National People's Congress, 10 to 15 percent of Tibetans were imprisoned, and of those imprisoned, 40 percent died as a result.[14] According to Amnesty International, between 1987 and 1992 there were more than 150 occasions in Lhasa when Tibetans were repressed during demonstrations.[15] Particularly devastating was the spring of 1989 (two months before the Beijing massacre), when the Chinese Communists orchestrated a massive repression in Lhasa and proclaimed martial law. Tang Daxian, a

Chinese journalist with the *Beijing Youth Journal*, who was in Lhasa at the time, has published an article abroad based on his own observations and the evidence he collected at the time. According to his figures, about four hundred Tibetans were massacred, roughly one thousand were injured, and more than three thousand were arrested.[16]

In a speech at Yale University the Dalai Lama said that 1.2 million Tibetans had died of starvation or persecution during the years of Chinese Communist rule in Tibet.[17] The Tibetan government-in-exile has compiled the following statistics: between 1949 and 1979, 170,000 Tibetans died while imprisoned; 160,000 received a capital sentence; 430,000 were killed in armed clashes with the Chinese; 340,000 died of starvation; 100,000 either committed suicide or were killed in a "political struggle."[18] If these figures are correct, it means that the total deaths equaled one-sixth of the entire population of Greater Tibet.[19]

The Tibetans are also deprived of their right to own property. The Chinese government compelled the Tibetans to participate in the socialist movement, a process that left Tibetans more impoverished than ever. In 1980 Hu Yaobang, the Party head who best understood Tibet, conducted an inspection mission to the region. In the face of the severe poverty he encountered, Hu later asked (in a meeting of the Tibet Autonomous Region Communist Party Committee): "Has all the Chinese government's aid been thrown into the Yalong Zangbu River?" Ren Rong, the general secretary of the Tibet Autonomous Region Communist Party Committee, was expelled from his post and was succeeded by Yin Fatang, who soon admitted that Tibet was suffering from "extreme poverty."[20] Hu Yaobang proclaimed that Tibet must return to the level of living standards that had been achieved before the Communists had ousted the Tibetan government in 1959.

Since the implementation of China's economic reforms, Tibet's standard of living has risen somewhat, compared to the conditions Hu witnessed in 1980. According to those knowledgeable about the region, however, the wealthier people in Tibet are predominantly Chinese. Because business and other activities depend on personal and political connections, and since it is the Chinese who have such connections, Tibetans have difficulty competing. It is reported that, in the main shopping area of Bakhor, Chinese shop owners far outnumber Tibetans.

Even worse than economic deprivation has been religious persecution. According to the figures compiled by the Tibetan government-in-exile, as of 1979, of the original 6,259 Tibetan monasteries, the majority had been completely destroyed and only eight monasteries remained largely intact. Of the original 590,000 monks, 110,000 had been persecuted or killed, and 250,000 were forced to resume secular life.[21] Today, religious persecution is not so pervasive as before, but the Tibetans still do not enjoy religious freedom. All Tibetan monasteries and monks are under the control of the Chinese United Front and the Religion Committees. Rigid rules have been laid down governing who can become a monk: "Anyone eighteen or over who loves China and loves the Communist Party [can enter the order]. His parents must consent. After entering a monastery, he must learn Marxism and realize that materialism and idealism are opposing worldviews."

Monks expressing dissatisfaction with these controls, particularly Tibetans who advocate independence, are often arrested. According to formerly imprisoned Tibetans, to compel confessions the Chinese use various forms of torture, such as electric batons, gun butts, and steel rods. They also use cigarette butts to cause burns and dogs that are trained to bite. "There are thirty-three methods of torture used in Tibet," according to a former security bureau officer who had been stationed in Tibet and who is now in exile in the West.[22]

Even for a Chinese who has not lived in Tibet, one who has lived under the control of the Communist government can well imagine China's repressive practices. But the Tibetans have had to endure something that the Chinese have not. While under the despotic rule of the Communists, the Tibetans have suffered racial discrimination. In an essay that appears elsewhere in this volume, Wei Jingsheng, one of the best-known Chinese dissidents, writes that, although his parents had never met any Tibetans, when they learned that his girlfriend was a Tibetan, they opposed their relationship and threatened to disown him. His father opposed their relationship because he thought Tibetans were "half human and half animal."[23] This type of thinking is the result of years of Chinese communist propaganda.

## Which Is More important: Unification or Human Freedom?

The Chinese have many "reasons" to believe that preserving a Greater China is paramount and thus to oppose Tibetan independence. One of the excuses is that, if Tibet were to became independent, Xinjiang and Inner Mongolia would follow Tibet's example, which would lead to the disintegration of China's territorial mass. No one wants to assume that responsibility. But what should really be the starting point for our thinking on this subject, the nation or the individual? What is more important, unification of the empire or individual freedom? Let us compare two hypothetical situations:

The first would be the resurrection today of Vladimir Lenin and of the former Soviet Union. By using military force, Lenin would revive communism, unify all the fifteen former Soviet republics and reestablish the USSR. All the people in the USSR would be subjugated, but the country would be unified. The second scenario would be for the former Soviet Union to remain disintegrated as fifteen independent countries. The Soviet Union would no longer exist, but the people would have freedom. Which situation would the people choose? Actually we already know the answer. The people of the former USSR chose the latter course. Why do the Chinese stubbornly insist on unification, even when the result is an inability to exercise their will freely?

Concepts of boundary and nation are not ultimate values.

Among the provisions of the 1975 Helsinki Accord (officially, the Final Act of the Conference on Security and Cooperation in Europe) was one that permitted changes to nation-state boundaries through peaceful means. The spirit of the accord is that boundaries are not necessarily permanent. Individual freedom and wishes outweigh any concerns of boundaries. This is a simple principle. Boundaries, a nation's form, and its social system are all human constructs. Their starting point and ultimate purpose are freedom and dignity. When boundaries or social systems are not harmonious with the people's needs or are contrary to the will of the majority, it is better to change them than to twist people's "needs" to suit some nationalistic imperative.

Those who worry about the domino effect—i.e., the theory that if Tibet becomes independent, then Xinjiang and Inner Mongolia will also seek independence—often ask what would happen if the other twenty-nine provinces all wanted to become independent. But the conditions do not exist for this. The problem with this theoretical problem is its impossibility. Before people declare independence, certain conditions must exist. For example, they must have a distinct ethnicity or culture, or at least a common history as an independent nation-state, which the majority is seeking to reestablish.

Normally there is a rational basis for seeking independence. For example, when the USSR split into the present fifteen states, Russia's population and size exceeded that of the other fourteen nation-states. But there is no talk of splitting Russia proper into even smaller nations. (Chechnia comprises a completely different ethnic group.) The most important reason for this is that Russians are mostly of the same ethnicity, share the same culture, and over the past several hundred years have no history of splitting up. More to the point, virtually all Russians wish to remain united as one country. Only when they attempt to subjugate other nationalities, such as the Chechens, is there trouble.

Similarly, the Japanese once established Manchukuo in Northeastern China. Yet the people in those three provinces do not ask for independence. The fear of the domino effect is comparable to the fear that if the United States lets in one refugee from China, then all the 1.2 billion Chinese will want to come. People who create such straw men—use foolish, unrealistic assumptions—are in effect depriving the weak and the oppressed of certain rights.

Placing more importance on matters of nationalism than on individual freedom and dignity has a long history in China. The entire five thousand years of our history has emphasized collective values, such as nationalism, collective society, and imperial rule, over individual freedom. The core of Chinese culture, which the Confucianists and their followers established, can be summed up as subordination of the individual will to the collective will. Many well-known Chinese intellectuals in recent history, including Kang Youwei, Liang Qichao, Chen Duxiu, Zhang Taiyan, and Liang Shuming, have urged reforms to make China a strong country, but rarely did they mention individual rights and freedoms. Even Yan Fu, the translator of John Stuart Mill's *On Liberty,* who wanted to introduce the Chinese to Western philosophies of freedom and liberty, viewed these theories merely as a means of achieving a more powerful nation, and not as a goal in themselves. In the nearly half-century of Chinese Communist rule, national values have been given even more emphasis. Through intense and systematic exposure to this line of nationalism, the Chinese people have been brainwashed. It is evident from the democracy movements in recent years that nationalism and patriotism had been the dominant themes. For example, whether it is the April 5 (1976) movement or the 1989 democracy movement, the inevitable theme at Tiananmen Square has always been nationalism and patriotism. The Tiananmen student leaders pleaded for the government's recognition of the movement as "patriotic." We hardly heard any appeal for individualism.

This thinking is not limited to liberals. As China has grown economically, some Chinese intellectuals have introduced the doctrine of "neo-authoritarianism." The essence of this doctrine is still traditional Chinese thinking, that is, national interest takes precedence over individual rights and social collective order is still more important than individual freedom.

Ironically, in spite of the five thousand years of believing that a powerful nation is of the utmost importance, China is still weak. The basic reason is that the Chinese, particularly Chinese intellectuals, have transposed the values of individual freedom and national strength. The result is that the people are not free, nor is the nation powerful.

**Who Should Decide Tibet's Future?**

Some say that whether or not Tibet should be independent is up to the Chinese rather than to the Tibetans themselves. But is it right for this decision to be left to the Chinese? Then there are others who do allow that the decision should be left to both the Tibetans and the Chinese. But this would also deny the Tibetans of their right to self-determination. The reason is simple: There are more than one billion Chinese and only six million Tibetans. If the Chinese population did not increase and the Tibetan population were to rise at 3 percent annually (the highest rate worldwide), it would still take fifteen hundred years before the Tibetans reached the same population as the Chinese. Thus Tibetans would essentially be deprived of a voice in this matter.

On the Tibet issue, the meaning of "respecting the majority's will" has to mean respecting the majority of the *Tibetan* people's will. However, independence is not the most important value, just as unification and national strength are not the most important goals. The most important requirement is respect for the Tibetans' right to self-determination. It should not matter to the Chinese whether they choose self-rule or unification with China.

In 1993 Puerto Rico held a national vote on whether it should become the fifty-first state of the United States. This case exemplifies a respect for the doctrine of self-determination. Whether or not Puerto Rico should be unified with the United States was up to the people of Puerto Rico, not the Americans in the fifty states. If this decision had been placed in the hands of people of the United States, with its population of 250 million, Puerto Rico, with a population of 3 million, would have in effect been deprived of its right to determine its own destiny. The U.S. government and the American people did not interfere but respected the wishes of the Puerto Rican people.[24]

According to U.S. law, however, if the majority of Puerto Ricans had chosen to become the fifty-first state of the United States, they still could not automatically do so; such a step would have to be approved by the U.S. Congress. In other words, if Puerto Rico wanted independence, only a vote for independence by the majority of Puerto Ricans is needed; if Puerto Rico wanted to become the fifty-first state, a majority vote of the American people is needed. This is similar to good family relations. For example, if one spouse requests a divorce, the court hears the dispute and may grant the divorce decree. A consensus from both parties is not needed. But if one spouse does not want the divorce and seeks to restore the relationship, that spouse must have the consent of the other spouse. Divorce requires only one party, whereas marriage requires the consent of both parties. For another example, consider a large family with many brothers. If one brother wants to move out, the decision is his alone. But if the same brother wants to return to the family home, the majority of the brothers in the house must approve.

**Tibet and the Security of China**

Some Chinese "realists" stress that were Tibet to become independent this would threaten China's national security. China and India have fought border wars. Located astride the Himalayas, they often eye each other warily. "Realists" argue that India's army would penetrate an independent Tibet and threaten the security of China because there would be no buffer between China and Tibet.

This assumption not only ignores the will and wishes of the Tibetans but also overlooks their tradition of peace. In recent history Tibet has suffered attacks from foreign forces, including the Chinese Qing dynasty and the British. The Tibetans are now under the control of the Chinese government. What is the basis for assuming that the Indian army would conquer Tibet? Tibet's exiled government and more than 100,000 Tibetan refugees have already lived in India for thirty-seven years; although they are on Indian territory, the Indians let the Tibetans manage their own affairs. The exiled government and the Tibetan community have always enjoyed India's respect and noninterference.

During a speech to the U.S. Congress in 1987, the Dalai Lama set forth a "Five-point Peace Plan" concerning the Tibet issue.[25] One of the points called for the demilitarization of Tibet as well as for Tibet to be recognized as an environmentally protected region. If Tibet became a demilitarized region this would benefit the security of both China and India because if either India or China attempted military actions against the other, they would first have to go through Tibet. Not only would this be opposed by the Tibetans, but it would also attract international condemnation. It would not be as it is now, where China and India can start fighting at any time precisely because Tibet is not a buffer zone. How could a demilitarized Tibet led by the Dalai Lama, Nobel peace prize winner and advocate of nonviolence, threaten either country?

## Can Tibet Survive without China's "Help"?

In discussing Tibet, many Chinese also stress a point that the Chinese government has often reiterated, namely, that Tibet used to have a system of slavery and was poor and backward. Through economic aid from China, Tibet's standard of living has risen. This point was also noted in the *White Paper* on Tibet's human rights, published by the Chinese government to prove that "without the Communists, there would be no new Tibet."

What is the truth? First, the accuracy of the figures used in the White Paper are in question. As of now, China does not have freedom of the press. If the figures are not subject to independent auditing and the government does not allow room for dispute, how reliable can such figures be? Even if all of them are accurate, after forty-seven years could a nation not have made some improvements? Who can be sure that Tibet would not be better off if China had not intervened?

Second, although no one denies that Tibet's earlier system of serfdom was backward, is military intervention permitted to force reform in other nations?

Third, can we really say that had it not been for the Communists there would be no "new" Tibet? The reality of this painful past half-century tells us that just as Communist rule has brought great suffering to the Chinese people, so it was with the Tibetans. Furthermore, the belief that Tibet cannot survive without China's aid is based on prejudice and belittles the intelligence of the Tibetans; it is condescending as well. The Tibetans in India have not only established their own government, they also have a constitution that was voted on by the exiled Tibetans. The constitution guarantees freedom of expression, freedom of the press, and the right to own property. Robert Thurman, professor of Indo-Tibetan studies at Columbia University, has stated: "His Holiness reconstructed a viable Tibetan community in India, preserving the culture of Tibet. He held the Tibetan people together in exile and gave them hope during the very severe, even genocidal, oppression in their homeland. He is also the first leader of Tibet to become a world leader, even without [direct access to] a political base—just on his moral force."[26] The exiled Tibetans now live under India's roof; yet, even under these circumstances, they have been able to establish an independent, prosperous, and democratic society. Would they lose this ability if Tibet became independent?

Some argue that because Tibet has not industrialized, Chinese aid will be necessary for the region to develop. However, the people of Mongolia are herdsmen and had little industry, and yet they have been able to develop. It is true that they used to receive Soviet aid, but they did not have to be incorporated into the USSR to receive it. With the fall of the USSR, Mongolia is no longer communist, and the people not only are free but have grown more prosperous than ever. Regardless of nationality or race, as long as a people have freedom, they can achieve greatness. That is the most significant point, and the Chinese should not hold on to the communist notion that communism is everyone's savior.

The most basic principles for resolving the Tibet question are respect for self-determination and recognition of individual freedom. National boundaries and types of social systems do not determine whether there will be individual freedom and rights. In this spirit we must respect Tibet's right to freedom. The Tibetans have the right to define their own nation, adopt their own culture and way of life, select their own social system, and elect their own leader. All these matters are for the Tibetans to work out, not the Chinese.

The Chinese have always stressed nationalism. Tibet is also a case where nationalism is appropriate. We Chinese, with our population of more than one billion, can take little pride in having intimidated the weaker Tibetans. Chinese intellectuals in particular should feel ashamed that they have remained silent or even chimed in with the official propaganda in the face of this oppression. In modern Chinese history, China has been threatened and humiliated by foreign forces. China is now threatening and humiliating a weaker nationality. This will prove to be a shameful page in China's history, particularly in the Han people's history. I call on my fellow Chinese to repent. There will be a time in the future when these crimes are judged.

**Notes**

1. China's Center for Tibetology and China's Second Historical Archives, comps., *A Collection of the Documents of the Funeral Ceremony of the Thirteenth Dalai Lama and the Enthronement of the Fourteenth Dalai Lama* (Shisan shi dalai yuanji zhiji he shisi shi dalai zhuanshi zuochuang dang'an xuanbian) (Beijing: China's Tibetology Publishing House, 1990). Hereafter, *Collection*.

2. *Tibet—Its Ownership and Human Rights Situation* (Beijing: Information Office of the State Council, 1992). Hereafter, *White Paper*.

3. Ya Hanzhang, *Biographies of the Dalai Lamas* (Beijing: People's Publishing House, 1984), p. 21.

4. Ya, *Biographies*, p. 21.

5. *Collection.*
6. Ya, *Biographies*, p. 329.
7. Ibid., p. 330.
8. *Tibet Daily*, August 27, 1989.
9. *Collection*, Official letter No. 439.
10. Ibid., Official letter No. 441.
11. Ya, *Biographies*, p. 34.
12. *White Paper.*
13. John F. Avedon, *In Exile from the Land of Snows* (Chinese edition) (Taiwan: Huiju Publishing House, 1991), p. 134. In 1962 a Tibetan guerrilla army attacked the Chinese army on the road from Xinjiang to Lhasa, killing the commanding officer and some official advisers. They also captured a book, *Basic Teaching Materials of Tibet Condition Education*, written by the Political Department of Tibet Military Region. The book says: "Between March and October in 1959, [the Chinese army] wiped out eighty-seven thousand Tibetan rebels."
14. Daniel Southerland, "Mass Death in Mao's China," *Washington Post*, July 17, 1994.
15. Ministry of Foreign Affairs and Department of News of the Tibetan Government-in-Exile, *The Truth about Tibet* (Chinese edition), 1993 ed., p. 20.
16. Tang Daxian, *Report of the Lhasa Event in 1989*, in *Democracy in China* [U.S.] (August 1991), p. 33.
17. The Dalai Lama's speech at Yale University, October 9, 1991, published by *Democracy in China* [Tokyo] (September 1993).
18. *The Truth about Tibet*, p. 19.
19. According to the *White Paper*, the fourth census of China in 1990 put the Tibetan population at 4,590,000. According to research by the Chinese scholar Huan Xiang, published in *Beijing Comment* (February 1988), "Tibet has six million people; one-third live in the Tibet Autonomous Region, the others live in other provinces." According to Tibetan government-in-exile's *The Truth of Tibet*, the total population of Greater Tibet is six million.
20. The article by Yin Fatang, *Red Flag*, no. 8 (1983).
21. This was confirmed by the Tenth Panchen Lama in 1988. During a meeting of China's Center of Tibetology in Beijing, he said, "All the monasteries where Tibetans live have been destroyed. The remaining seven or eight are not totally intact."
22. *The Truth about Tibet*, p. 21.
23. Wei Jingsheng, "A Letter to Deng Xiaoping," *Beijing Spring* [New York] (1994), p. 59. [Translated from the Chinese original in the present volume.—Eds.]
24. The result of the citizens' vote was that the majority in Puerto Rico wanted to preserve the status quo as a commonwealth, and become neither independent nor a state of the United States.
25. The Dalai Lama, "Five-point Peace Plan for Resolving the Tibet Problem," *Democracy in China* [Japan] (June 1994), p. 33.
26. Claudia Dreifus, "Interview with the Dalai Lama," *New York Times Magazine*, November 28, 1993, p. 52.

# Brainwashing the Chinese

## Cao Changching

When the government holds absolute control of the media, the government can easily manipulate the facts and dominate the interpretation of history. Under the Communist's endless one-sided propaganda, the people's thinking about the Tibetan issue is now on the same track as the Communist's propaganda machine. Thus whenever Chinese discuss the issue, chauvinism and nationalism predominate.

Under the present dictatorship, historical truthfulness gets short shrift. What is "important" is whether historical interpretation satisfies government ideology. Even Ya Hanzhang, an official Chinese Tibetan "authority," wrote in the foreword of *Biographies of Dalai Lamas* that the book was meant to satisfy "the needs of the struggle," the agenda having been set by "the Party." Ya Hanzhang's admission epitomizes books on Tibet published in China since the Communists took over: Historical "truth" must correspond to the Party line.

Books published on Tibet always maintain the same tone. In May 1993 the Beijing Huaqiao Publishing House put out a book called *Modern History of Tibet* (Xizang fengyun lu), which unabashedly declared that the Chinese government had brought heaven to the Tibetans. For example, concerning the completion in 1954 of the roads from Sichuan and Qinghai to Lhasa, this book claimed that "the entire world is amazed, the whole of humanity has undergone a sense of change, and the whole world is looking to the ancient world peak perched in the east." Regarding Tibet after the 1959 repression (during which more than eighty thousand Tibetans were massacred), this book stated that the Communists established "an unprecedented paradise," adding that "Tibet has undergone many vast, miraculous changes."

The Chinese people have received their knowledge about Tibet from these highly politicized "studies." It is difficult for Western and Tibetan scholars to publish their Tibetan research in China, inasmuch as their books are not in accordance with the Beijing government's view. An exception was the book by American journalist John. F. Avedon, *In Exile from the Land of Snows*, based on four years of research and hundreds of interviews. The book was translated into Chinese and published by the official Tibetan Publishing Company in March 1988. Immediately upon publication in Lhasa, the book sold out. Its content immediately became a hot topic of discussion. Almost all college students in Lhasa read the book, which most found more credible than the Chinese propaganda they had been fed. But not long after the book's appearance the government stopped its distribution and actually confiscated copies that had already been sold. An "Emergency Notice" declared that the distribution of this book had been "an error."

If books on Tibet published by the Chinese government were truthful, the government need not fear being challenged. The Chinese government's prohibition of heterodox books only illustrates the fact that the Chinese government's propaganda about Tibet is false, because honesty is never afraid of being challenged.

Of course it is not just a matter of a half-century of brainwashing. Traditional Chinese chauvinism and nationalism have further provided a foundation for the Chinese people to accept the Communists' point of view on Tibet. But the propaganda has left an added impression in the minds of the Chinese people. For example, one of my friends, an official in the Chinese government, once came to see me when she was in New York on business. I gave her a Chinese translation of a book by the Dalai Lama. Surprised, she pointed to the cover of the book and said, "His smile is so sincere and loving." She had never seen the

Dalai Lama's picture before! From the government propaganda she had heard that the Dalai Lama was engaged in "splittist" activities; in her mind he was evil and fierce. After reading his book she was moved by his philosophy of love, his compassion, and his human responsibility. When she was about to return to China, she asked me for another copy of the book, which she took back to Beijing and gave to her best friend.

The changes in my own view on the Tibetan issue are somewhat similar to her experience. After graduating from college I worked as a journalist. The "knowledge" I then possessed about Tibet had been totally instilled by the government. Even though I viewed Tibet as a remote and totally unfamiliar place, I had never doubted that it was a part of China. It was only after coming to the United States and reading the works of Western scholars, and some by unbiased Chinese and Tibetans, that I realized that the Chinese government's view on Tibet was one-sided. As on so many subjects, regarding both the history of Tibet and its present situation the Chinese government had simply lied.

So I always tell friends who have just come from China that they must be aware that their "knowledge" has been instilled by the government; that is, they must consider their brain as a computer and reevaluate its "software," often installing new programs and real truths. Unfortunately many have not attached importance to this essential task. Even those who are inclined to be skeptical of Party propaganda think that as soon as they arrive in the West the truth will automatically reveal itself to them. In fact no matter where we move our "computers," the old software lives on unless we take the initiative to replace it with updated versions.

The impact of the communist "software" can be seen from the recent essays about Tibet published by Xu Mingxu, a so-called Tibetan scholar from China. Xu has already lived in the United States for several years, but his essays are full of communist logic. For example, in his "Tibetan Independence Is the Doomsday of a Democratic China" (*Beijing Spring* [New York, 1995]),

Xu not only reiterated the government views expressed in the official Chinese document, *Tibet—Its Ownership and Human Rights Situation*, he went on to support the Chinese government's continuance of its tough line with the Tibetans. He continued to use the harsh Chinese communist tone, stating, "Anyone who has been to Tibet would realize that the Tibetans now have full religious freedom." Is this not like China's Department of Propaganda—lying without batting an eye?

From the time China occupied Tibet until now, when have the Tibetans ever experienced full religious freedom? Given the widespread deprivation and violation of the *Chinese* people's religious freedom, why would anyone think that the Chinese Communists made an exception and gave the *Tibetans* full religious freedom? And to say that "anyone who has been to Tibet would realize . . ." is simply untrue. I have read essays by Western scholars who visited Tibet who stated that the Tibetans' religious freedom has been seriously violated. Xu also contradicts himself in the same essay by admitting that "Tibetans, like the Chinese, have no freedom of expression, publication, assembly, and association." Can there be a place in this world where the people have freedom of religion and at the same time lack freedom of expression, publication, assembly, and association? Does this conform to basic logic or common sense? Xu also equated the Chinese government's military repression of Tibetans in Lhasa in the spring of 1989 with the police actions in the 1992 Los Angeles riots. Xu believes both were necessary. This is absurd. This kind of logic can only come from people whose brains are filled with communist "software."

Xu's views on Tibet reflect the fact that the communist "software" stubbornly continues to function in the minds of overseas Chinese. It would be better for these people to install the "software of truth" than to fervently promote the "software of lies." That would be refreshing. It can be exhausting to bear the burden of lies in a world where truthful information is freely circulated!

Of course people who share Xu's opinion can argue that they are not supporters of the Chinese government because they themselves are also victims of a communist dictatorship. On many occasions Xu has made statements about his own victimization. "Because I once published novels exposing the corruption of the Chinese government, for many years I was banished, exiled to Tibet." But is a victim of persecution necessarily more correct than his oppressor? In view of his personal experience, how can we account for Xu's chauvinism? Milan Kundera, the Czech author who has observed the communist culture firsthand, has written an account of the problem. In his novel, *The Farewell Party*, he speaks through the voice of Jakub, the protagonist: "I'll tell you the saddest discovery of my life. The victims are no better than their oppressor. I can easily imagine their roles reversed." This same phenomenon can be seen in China today. Deng Xiaoping was persecuted by Mao Zedong on three occasions, but the June 4, 1989, massacre conducted by Deng reveals that he is no more compassionate than Mao. To determine whether a person acts in the right way depends not on whether that person is the victim or the oppressor; what matters are whether the values and perspectives of the victim are more humane than those of the oppressor. One can see from Xu's essays that despite his persecution under the Chinese Communists, his values have much in common with them. In his opinion, nationalism, collectivism and national borders are higher values than individual freedom; if the two conflict, individual freedom must be sacrificed to the "national interest." It is obvious that the fundamental fault of communism all over the world is that it stresses collective values and deprives the individual of his or her right to choose. The result is that not only does the individual lack freedom, but, ironically, the nation is not strong either. The basic reason that Western civilization can triumph over Communism is that it puts individual freedom above all else.

Because of the many years of the Chinese government's denial of freedom, general persecution, and discrimination, Tibetans are angry at the Chinese. This is especially so among younger Tibetans. Voices demanding the use of violence to fight the Chinese are becoming stronger among the exiled young Tibetans in India.

The Dalai Lama has actually felt obliged to declare that if the Tibetans were to use violence he would resign from his present position in the Tibetan government-in-exile.

Inasmuch as almost all Chinese share their government's opinion about Tibet, it is not surprising that many Tibetans are portrayed as being somewhat unfriendly toward the Chinese. In March 1995 I attended the Tibetan New Year celebration in New York. That night I talked with about a dozen Tibetans. A young Tibetan told me, "If there was no reason, why should Tibetans dislike Chinese? The Chinese we have met all support China's occupation." His words reminded me of one of Mao Zedong's aphorisms, "Love is never without reason, nor is hate." As Chinese, should we not seriously consider why the Tibetans dislike us? If we had not so bullied the Tibetans, would there be hatred? Is there any among us who have hated someone for no reason? As long as there are people like Xu, who, whether inadvertently or not, zealously and stubbornly reflect Chinese government propaganda, how can Tibetans separate the Chinese people from the Chinese government?

Communist rule in China is coming to an end. This does not necessarily mean, however, that the Tibetan issue can be automatically resolved. It would be a blasphemy against freedom if, on the one hand, the Chinese insist on democracy and freedom for themselves but, on the other hand, did not respect the Tibetans' right to choose self-determination.

A young Tibetan once remarked to me: "When I am talking with Chinese about the June 4 massacre, we all criticize the Beijing government. But when I bring up the Tibetan issue, they immediately parrot the Chinese government. What kind of 'democracy' and 'freedom' do they have in mind?" What kind, indeed?

# Tibetans' Rights and Chinese Intellectuals' Responsibility

## Ding Zilin and Jiang Peikun

The Chinese People's Liberation Army (PLA) made its initial foray into Tibet at the end of 1949. Under this pressure Tibet sent a delegation to sign a "Seventeen-point Agreement" with the Chinese government. This agreement permitted the PLA to complete its takeover of the region. The Chinese government called this "Tibet's peaceful liberation."

In 1959 there was an uprising in Tibet against Chinese rule, which was repressed by the PLA. Eighty thousand Tibetans were "eliminated," and the Fourteenth Dalai Lama fled to India accompanied by 100,000 followers. The Chinese government referred to its action as "putting down a rebellion."

Thereafter, almost all Tibetan monasteries were destroyed. Although seven or eight monasteries escaped destruction, none has been left unscathed. According to the late Panchen Lama, of the original 600,000 Tibetan monks, 110,000 died because of persecution and 250,000 were forced to convert [to secular life]. The Chinese government dismisses this great calamity as just another phenomenon of the Cultural Revolution.

In the spring of 1989 Lhasans protested. The Chinese military and police forcefully repressed their protest and imposed martial law. During this incident, numerous Tibetans were injured or killed and many were arrested and imprisoned. The Chinese government again referred to this as "putting down a rebellion."

The number of Tibetans killed for political or religious reasons during the almost half-century of "peace" is unknown, as is the number who starved to death. But if we consider the millions of people who have died from unnatural causes in the last few decades in China, obviously Tibet must have had a high mortality rate.

During the occupation of Tibet, hardly any of China's 1.2 billion people has spoken up on behalf of the Tibetans or expressed compassion for their tragedies. There are a few exceptions, including such Chinese leaders as Hu Yaobang and a few of the dissidents, such as Wei Jingsheng. Unfortunately, though, almost all Chinese people have silently accepted the Chinese government's repression of the Tibetans and the deprivation of the Tibetans' right to self-determination. Most Chinese actually believe China's propaganda regarding Tibet, and almost no one has seriously contemplated what they have been fed. The issues are difficult to understand because our Chinese minds have been transformed by the Chinese government and have become numb. Thus, in the spring of 1989, when the largest democracy demonstration in China's history erupted in Beijing, no one was heard in Tiananmen Square speaking up for the Tibetans. Participants in that movement seemed unaware that just two months earlier Tibet had suffered a bloody massacre at the hands of the Chinese authorities.

History has its ironies. During the 1989 Tiananmen demonstrations we heard from the foreign media that Tibet's spiritual leader, the Dalai Lama, had made a statement saluting those who sacrificed their lives for freedom, human rights, and democracy for the Chinese people. We were moved by this, but at the same time we were saddened and felt guilty. What could we say? Forty years had passed and those of us who believed we still had a conscience had never been aware of our responsibility to support the Tibetans in their struggle for human rights. Even when faced with the Tibetans' sufferings, we still acted with indifference. But during the days of *our* distress, we received the Tibetan leader's support. Though the voice came from afar, it warmed our hearts.

We now realize that we Chinese cannot remain insensitive. We must view history without bias; we must reconsider the Tibetan issue without ideological blinders. We must also change our manner toward the Tibetans and treat them as equals.

For a long time the "collective consciousness" of most Chinese, especially us Hans, has been misguided; we refer to the notion that Tibet undoubtedly belongs to China. People seem to think that any governmental conduct, no matter how repressive, is above criticism as long as the government is acting to preserve China's so-called territorial integrity. So they believe that it is incumbent on them to oppose the Tibetans' demand for independence, even their demand for democratic freedoms. This deeply rooted collective consciousness has made a majority of the Chinese people remain awfully reticent in the face of the Chinese government's brutal repression and persecution of the Tibetans.

It is not for us to decide whether Tibet is a part of the Chinese territory; this can be determined only by history. The problem is that the Chinese government has instructed historians to falsify Tibet's history in order to validate its domination of Tibet and thus to instill in the minds of the Chinese people the idea of China's sovereignty over Tibet. The Chinese government has used this method to repress dissenting views on the sovereignty of Tibet and to deprive the Tibetans of their right to determine their own sociopolitical system.

In the past forty-odd years, the Chinese government has always followed the theory that the country's "unification" is of paramount importance and that individual freedom and rights are insignificant. They use these theories not only to deprive and trample on the Tibetans' right to a national self-determination, but to resist criticism of their policies toward Tibet from the international community, especially criticism of their human rights record in Tibet. The Chinese government disseminates unending propaganda abroad to the effect that Tibet once had a brutal system of serfdom, with people living under terrible conditions. They go on to claim that the Communists liberated one million serfs and that socialism ensured that the Tibetans could leave behind their former poverty and backwardness. Of course no one today would deny the backwardness and poverty of the old order, or that the Tibetans' living standards are somewhat better than before. Even so, must the cost of progress be the loss of life and freedom?

Although it might appear that it was with the "aid" of the Communists that "serfdom" was overthrown, what has really been accomplished for these people? Must Tibetans be treated like livestock in exchange for their subsistence? Must Tibetans behave like slaves in exchange for their freedom? What kind of logic is this? How silly it all sounds!

[What has happened to the Tibetans] is irrefutable, brutal reality. To say that the Communists helped the Tibetans to extricate themselves from backwardness and poverty is empty propaganda. In fact socialism no more brought prosperity to the Tibetans than it did to us Chinese. Despite the economic reforms, the wealthy people in Tibet are primarily Chinese, not Tibetans. Anyway, people cannot be expected to live like animals, with no demands other than to have enough to eat and wear. Do not forget that Tibet was originally a theocracy situated on this piece of land; it was religion alone that formed the basis of their nation's cultural tradition. The Tibetans' quest for religious spirituality far exceeds their quest for material things. For the Tibetans, the demand for religious freedom is a demand for political freedom. The Dalai Lama, as their spiritual leader, is also their political leader. It should not be ignored that in recent years the protests and demonstrations in Lhasa sprang primarily from religious circumstances and that the participants included monks and nuns. This shows that the Tibetans' demand for political freedom has been fueled by religion.

The Chinese government has always used the pledge of economic development and improved quality of life to repress the Chinese people's political demands. At the same time the Chinese government has used this pledge to repress the Tibetans' political and religious demands. But all this has not eliminated their demand for independence and national self-determination.

In the almost half-century of disaster, it has already become clear to the Tibetans that as long as the Chinese government continues to preserve its dictatorship and autocracy in Tibet, just as it does in China proper, none of their religious and political demands can be realized. If the Tibetans are to control their own fate, they have no choice but to struggle.

The decade-long quest for national self-determination and religious and political freedom, and the extent of Tibet's difficulties, are not generally appreciated in today's world; yet these difficulties should receive the world's sympathy and respect. The Dalai Lama's principles of a peaceful and nonviolent struggle should especially receive the world's approval and praise. As to Tibet's future, we have no reason to be pessimistic. But Tibet's future will depend on the Tibetans' continual struggle, as well as on the support of the Chinese people and the world community. As Chinese, we should not forget that in 1989 (a year that made righteous people indignant, suffocated, and afraid), Tibetans and Chinese waged similar struggles for freedom and dignity; their blood was shed on this same earth. We must bear this in mind. If they remember this, the Chinese people will understand that the gun that is aimed at the Tibetans is also aimed at the Chinese.

> May the Chinese people cast away past pride;
> May the Chinese people forgo yesterday's numbness;
> May the Chinese people and the Tibetans walk hand in hand
> For China's tomorrow;
> For Tibet's tomorrow.

*April 21, 1995*
*China's southern countryside*

# Tibetan, Chinese, and Human Rights

## Fang Lizhi

*The following is from an address the author gave in 1991 at a conference in New York.*

Ladies and gentlemen:

I am happy to address you at this conference on China and Tibet.

I will start with the answers to five questions that were sent to me by a journalist who wanted to know my views on Tibet for a book he was writing. His five questions were simple and direct, and they made me think about Tibet, China, democracy, the future, and, most important, whether when change eventually comes in China, as I believe it will, Tibetans and Chinese will still be able to find a way to live together in harmony.

Tibet has suffered much during the years of Chinese Communist Party rule, as has all of the People's Republic of China. But Tibet's cultural and religious life has been more severely attacked by the Communist Party than the traditions of the Han culture. Still, Tibetan culture has managed to survive; it seems to have great resilience.

Even though many Tibetans see the Hans as being responsible for the destruction of Tibetan culture and religion, mutual respect is still strong on a personal level between fair-minded people of the two races. For example, I have met a number of couples—one Han, one Tibetan. I myself had a close colleague at the

Chinese University of Science and Technology who is Tibetan, and we frequently had discussions together. I have also met with the Dalai Lama on various occasions.

But on a national level, in the realm of politics in a huge nation like the People's Republic of China, I do not know whether under current conditions there can be this kind of mutual tolerance and understanding.

People have frequently asked me what kind of political system Tibet should have and what its relation to China should be. Should it be a province with more autonomy, part of a federation or even a looser confederation, or should Tibet become independent? My answer is simple: I think the Tibetan people should decide all this. I respect their right to determine their own future and choose their own path.

This brings me back to my central question, whether it is still possible that Tibetans and Hans can find ways to live in harmony after all that has happened. We all want democracy. But will democracy make interaction among various social groups more harmonious, or less? A change toward genuine democratization is a necessary condition for such harmony, but it is not a sufficient condition in itself. In other words, we need both democracy and human rights if we are to find a way to live together peacefully, but something more is needed.

The Chinese Communist Party has always suppressed nationalistic feelings among the ethnic groups that make up the People's Republic of China. Han nationalism is considered to be fine, but minority nationalism is labeled "splittism" and "counterrevolutionary." Just as in Eastern Europe and in the Soviet Union in past decades, communism has driven nationalisms underground. The Communist Party's solution to the problem of the various minorities is to cover up their sense of uniqueness, to forbid any expression of nationalism. This, in the long term, is no solution at all. As long as the one-party rule of the Communist Party lasts, ethnic conflict will continue.

Nationalism can be understood as the desire to be able to

express one's distinct identity and develop one's culture and traditions. Thus it can be a positive impetus toward change and a brighter future when it keeps people struggling against oppression. In this struggle, nationalism creates positive feelings of social cohesion and community solidarity.

But nationalism has a dark side, too. This has been played out throughout the world. We have seen the negative side of nationalism emerge in events in Eastern Europe, since the lid of communist rule was taken off the boiling kettle of age-old anger and mistrust. We can see what happens when the pressure, which has been applied for far too long, is eased. Finally things explode. We have seen this in places like Yugoslavia, Romania, Armenia, and Azerbaijan.

In this century nationalism has been the most frequent cause of war. Both world wars arose out of nationalism. More recently, Saddam Hussein invoked the "historical" borders of Iraq when he invaded Kuwait, though, as far as we know, his principal motive for that act of force was to save his country's ailing economy from ruination. Yet I believe we are presented today with a unique opportunity, despite the Gulf War and the troubling fighting in Yugoslavia. These two examples give us a sense of the type of problems that may await us in China and Tibet. We must seize every opportunity to handle the issue better.

When the Chinese Communist Party collapses, as I believe it inevitably will, we will essentially have two choices. Either we can strengthen the differences between us, emphasize our separateness—thus going to the opposite extreme of the suppression of nationalism as practiced by the communists—or we can try to see beyond our differences, go beyond the limitations of nationalism, and talk about what we have in common.

I believe the first option will only lead to more distrust and hatred. Obviously people should not be prevented from practicing their own religion, enjoying their own customs, or developing their own culture. But to live together we need to emphasize the universal truths and seek ways of working together.

I think we must not retreat into our separate corners and stare at each other suspiciously from a distance. We must create an environment in which we can continue to talk through the problems that come up and find solutions to them, rather than allowing them to fester. We must find universal standards that bring us together in agreement and fellowship.

This conference seems to be an indication that we have a chance to make that second choice, and therefore I find it a hopeful sign.

# Tibet: An Unavoidable Issue

## Shen Tong

In October 1989, the autumn after the June 4 massacre, I met the Fourteenth Dalai Lama. Arranged by some friends who were concerned about the future of China and Tibet, this meeting was my first with the Tibetan religious and exile movement leader.

My mood at the time was a mixture of curiosity and guilt.

### I

Soon after the 1989 massacre I had learned that the Dalai Lama had openly denounced the Chinese Communist Party's atrocities against its unarmed and peacefully protesting Chinese citizens. But later I came to know that, for a long time, both the methods and the scale of the Communist party's numerous suppressions of the Tibetan movement for independence and freedom were even more horrendous than those of the massacre in Beijing. For example, when the Chinese army suppressed the Tibet "rebellion" in 1959, more than eighty thousand Tibetans lost their lives and another one hundred thousand fled to India. From 1959 until today, an estimated one million Tibetans were killed or died as the result of Chinese misrule. Thousands of Chinese troops are permanently stationed in Tibet to deal with the independence movement, which is carried on by religious and secular dissident activists. Even in what the official Chinese news media called the new Tibetan "paradise," many Tibetans continue to risk their lives to flee and seek exile.

I also learned that, after the June 4 massacre, within the Dalai

Lama's exile government there were high-ranking officials who opposed his denunciation of the Chinese Communist party's action. Concerned about the strategies for negotiating with the Chinese Communists, they had hoped the Dalai Lama would remain silent. He did not. Speaking from his Buddhist conscience and compassion, the Dalai Lama announced his support of the Chinese student movement for human rights and democracy.

At that time I had just gone into exile, and my impression of the Dalai Lama—firmly shaped in China—was similar to the image portrayed in official Chinese propaganda. Thus I was shocked when I learned of his action and deeply moved by his open-mindedness. A feeling of guilt soon arose in me, for I had known next to nothing about the sufferings of the Tibetans.

After learning more about the human rights situation in Tibet, in 1990 I accepted a Tibetan friend's invitation to speak at an international conference on Tibet held in New York City. I recall that my guilt was so strong that I could not even bring myself to deliver my prepared speech. Instead, I simply expressed my personal sympathies for the Tibetan people and their miseries, as well as my deep regret and sincere apologies for what the Chinese Communist regime had perpetrated in Tibet since the 1950s.

Once I had spoken, I was much relieved. The auditorium was filled with excitement. Lamas in red and yellow robes, young Tibetans, and Westerners supporting Tibet and human rights all cheered and applauded me in response to my action. I only saw my step as a duty, now that I had learned the truth about Tibet. Many told me that it was the first time they had heard a Chinese speaking with this kind of an attitude. But, paradoxically, soon my relief disappeared and I once more felt the burden of the past because for the past several decades, the Chinese mainland government has abused fundamental human rights in the Tibetan region. Any Chinese who truly loves freedom cannot turn away from this issue. This is a matter of conscience, a matter that goes far beyond historical origins, cultural differences, legality, and policy discussions. Reason and conscience demand that we face this reality.

## II

Because of the Chinese government's successful suppression of information, for a long time we Chinese knew little about the situation in Tibet. But ignorance cannot be an excuse for neglecting the human rights of Tibetans and their religious status or for ignoring the more complex issue of Tibetan sovereignty.[1] Our only excuse is that our "right to know," an important precondition of any rational and conscientious choice, had been denied. In essence, official censorship made a responsible choice impossible.

What about those few Chinese who did know?

Among the Chinese insiders, a clique of policymakers of the current government took their stand on the Tibetan issue by stationing troops in Tibet, sending Chinese migrants there, abusing basic human rights, dumping nuclear waste, and implementing fundamental social, economic, and cultural changes in what had become, for all practical purposes, a colony.

Going along with the tide, many Chinese who were aware of the Tibet situation but neither belonged to nor benefited from the government, supported the official policy or acquiesced in it. As time went on, many came to regard "the return of Tibetan sovereignty to China" as a matter of course.

Among Chinese political dissidents at home and abroad who believe in the principle of freedom, there are two lines of thought: One is the sentiment of Chinese nationalism, the other is denial of responsibility.

The first tendency sprang from the inconsistencies between chauvinist sentiments, on the one hand, and the desire to promote freedom and the processes of rational and informed discourse, on the other. It was also a product of a deliberate forgetting of unpleasant facts and maybe a mentality of cowardice.

The second tendency was to turn from reality and responsibility, which can be summarized as an inclination to attribute the problems to the past, to the future, or to ignorance. The first of these attitudes assigns all the fault to the Chinese Communist Party and its history over the past several decades. The second claims that when democracy materializes in China, all problems—including Tibet—will be quickly solved. The third views Tibet, a poor frontier province of six million commoners, as an issue too insignificant to mention. And the fourth positions its proponents outside the situation and concludes that the Chinese—and the status of the Chinese nation—will not permit Tibet to break free. Thus all four attitudes seem to casually evade with ease the reality of the Tibet situation.

## III

Although conscience certainly requires us to face the issue of Tibetan human rights, when it comes to Tibetan sovereignty, perhaps no such immediate pressure exists. But can the four attitudes mentioned above really be a safe haven for avoiding the issue? Let us look at each of them more closely.

From a historical perspective, it is perfectly reasonable to blame the Chinese Communist Party. "Historical inevitability," however, cannot explain the escalation of the Sino-Tibetan conflict and the deepening of the Tibetan tragedy, which were totally the consequences of man-made policies. No public opinion poll or ballot was taken when those policies were adopted nor was a democratic polity in place to entrust the decision-making power of such matters to the Chinese Communists. Therefore, claiming the Chinese Communist Party as the transgressor is logical and inevitable. Still, a trial of criminals is not the same as healing the wounds left from the crime. The past, dead, cannot substitute for the living present. Finger-pointing, though easy, cannot solve the problem.

This excuse also disguises a deeper danger. Students of modern history understand the difference between politicians' words and deeds while in opposition and those spoken and done *while in power*. Although the opposition party often attributes injustices to the party in power, often this is only out of tactical considerations. Even if their arguments have a reasonable basis, it does not guarantee that, once in power, the opposition, without a reexamination of its own responsibility and policy, will not go down the same old path. In fact, so long as a particular issue is not the focal point of current affairs, the possibility that a new government would continue to neglect that issue or repeat old policies is very high. To avoid that issue in the present, therefore, may lead to a denial of duty in the future.

Let us turn to the second attitude: that the realization of democracy in China will be the solution for Tibet (a kind of worshiping of the omnipotence of democracy).

In abstract terms, the establishment and consolidation of a democratic polity assume certain minimal conditions of cultural, social, and economic development. But, more often than not, these prerequisites cannot solve such problems as religious and ethnic conflict, economic prosperity, or even individual freedom. There is a sense that these issues belong to other spheres that are fundamentally apolitical. Specifically, achieving a stable democracy in China will undoubtedly require a long process, during which the evolution of Chinese polity will not automatically change the nature of other issues, such as that of Tibet.

Even after a democratic system is established and stabilized, the solutions of ethnic issues, if the issues continue to exist, must be found in a more fundamental realm outside the core values of democracy.[2] Why? Because ethnic issues, though a group identity issue, today often invoke the heart of human beings' self-identification. They are more basic, or provocative, than those norms that only regulate the interpersonal interaction of individuals within the same voluntaristic group—which are the kind of norms on which today's democracies are empirically based. In fact the reality of ethnic conflict may well pose a question about the necessity of a coherent national consciousness for the stability of a democratic polity.[3]

One can see from recent years that waves of democratic movements worldwide cannot calm the undercurrents of ethnic conflicts. The relatively peaceful coexistence of different ethnic groups in early democracies, such as Switzerland and Belgium, obviously is not a product of democracy. It is plausible that other unique factors have played a role in certain historical periods in those countries.[4] At least in the short term, more newly democratized nations like India destroyed the old regime and unlocked the doors of suppression. Ethnic conflict and religious fanaticism, long repressed but highly energetic, now exploded with such potential that no force could stop them.

In the period after the cold war, with the demise of communism as a worldwide social practice, some enthusiasts proclaimed "the end of history"—liberal democracy had triumphed. But the ethnic cleansing in the postcommunist former Yugoslavia clearly shows the tremendous destructive force of ultranationalism. With the pressure of the old empire taken away, "awakenings" of ethnic consciousness in the global waves of national self-determination and cultural relativism have caused new wounds and reopened historic ones.

Even if China, while in the process of implementing democracy, could at the same time construct a principle, or a new notion, of peaceful coexistence that would mitigate ethnic conflict, the realization of this principle would depend on bilateral (or multilateral) goodwill, not on the assumption that the Tibetan people would automatically accept such a principle. A peaceful solution does not necessarily take the form of the "heaven-and-earth-justified" dogma of "one great unification." This assumption is no different from the deceptive rationale of foreign invaders that their deeds were justified because the political system and economic aid they brought would benefit the place they invaded.

The third attitude, which regards the Tibetan issue as too insignificant to consider, is a blatant denial of reality and is self-deceptive. The gravity of Tibetan human rights problems aside, even the question of Tibetan sovereignty is extremely important within and beyond the current Chinese borders.[5] It is also quite an internationalized issue, which, on both symbolic and realistic terms, will seriously challenge any post–Deng Xiaoping Chinese central government. It is becoming increasingly clear that the costs of managing an empire are excessive.

Democracy advocates, for the time being, may not control or share any political power. Yet they have to respond positively to the issue of political determination and state clearly just when freedom of expression will be allowed to everyone, including the Tibetans.

Finally, let us look at the fourth attitude, one held by some ambitious Chinese would-be leaders: "objectively" commenting on or assessing the likelihood of China "allowing Tibetan self-determination"—and concluding negatively. I intend to discuss here neither the ambiguities of their concepts, such as "the status of the Chinese nation," in relation to the Tibetan issue nor the improprieties of the condescending attitude embodied in the term *allowing*. We must first respond to the Tibetan issue directly. Meanwhile, both the freedom fighters and the responsible intellectuals who are ready to take social action need to provide information to the general public and help it make its choice by presenting alternative values and frames of reference.

In sum, those four attitudes, emotionally or logically, cannot release us from our responsibility to face the Tibetan issue. Intellectuals cannot hide in any "safe haven," for such a haven turns out to be no more than a sand hill that covers an ostrich's head. Let us look clearly at Tibet and squarely face the issues of human rights and self-determination in those snow-covered mountains on the world's highest plateaus.

## IV

What we can see is a crude reality, suppressed, isolated, and undetected for a very long time, involving incessant brutality and vendetta, ruthless repression, and millions of broken families, refugees, and deaths.

When we try to look back in search of the origins of the issue of Tibetan sovereignty, history seems so elusive as to obscure any clear answer.[6] Straight answers require great courage and an open heart. Only genuine concern can help focus our attention and cut through illusion. Only true open-mindedness will enable us to accept and understand what evil has happened. Only real courage provides hope for those who are seeking truth in darkness.

The answer to the Tibetan issue lies neither in ancient Chinese, Tibetan, and Buddhist classics nor in the documentation of the rituals and customs of the intermarriages between the Chinese and Tibetan nobility. Isolated times and events—fragmented studies—are at best an end, never a beginning.

Rather, contemporary answers to the Tibetan issue will be found only in the Tibetan and Chinese people's sincere mutual trust, wisdom, and spirit of practicality. I do not intend, here, to address the issues of wisdom and practicality; that is ultimately the responsibility of those Chinese and Tibetans with actual power who, one hopes, will be truly insightful and influential. When the time comes, they are the ones who will have to take concrete action; who must be wise and practical when called on. The discussion of sincerity and trust can serve as the foundation for the consideration of our original attitude and a rational starting point in the search for answers to the Tibet question. Unfortunately the long-time separation and hostility between Tibetans and Chinese make immediate mutual trust nothing but a daydream. Nonetheless, it is both possible and necessary to establish a standard of common belief.

This common belief is the very core of the humanist value that can be described as respect for individuality and subsequently of basic human rights guaranteed by law. It is the negative freedom in the highly influential tradition of modern liberalism—freedom from impediments such as inhuman treatment with regard to life, thought, belief, and speech. This freedom is not based on the principle of the greatest happiness for the greatest number of people. Nor is it based on the abstract concept of the supremacy of national sovereignty and national interest. It does not presuppose the superiority of those few members of society who have the willpower or superior intelligence. It does not use analyses of social stratification and class struggle to deny the absoluteness and independence of the individual. It does not emphasize historicism to such an extent as to give up all other value systems. Nor does it promote absolutism by traditional, religious, and hereditary rights.[7] Instead, this liberalism stresses individual independence and the inviolable, inseparable, and inalienable individual freedoms, including the freedom from coercion and freedoms of life, thought, faith, and speech. This basic liberal principle has rich expressions in modern life. The revised and indispensable addition, after the principle of "the minority should obey the majority"—that "the majority should respect the minority"—is one example. Another is the expansion of the meanings of individual rights and the popularization of these ideas in people's awareness.

Closely associated with this liberal tradition, the modern polity, i.e., democracy, has its problems in pure theories. It is not prescribed, in an abstract and idealistic sense, as thoroughly and completely as various kinds of utopianism and romanticism. Yet until now this structure has proved to be the polity that protects, to the utmost possible extent, the above liberal principle in the actual practice of modern Western society.[8]

Nevertheless, this polity is built on a consensus: The whole society more or less recognizes the legitimacy of the state with its restrained power and exercise of rule of law; it periodically participates in the selection of the governing body, which changes on the basis of fixed terms; and it freely competes in the process of selection through free voting. When this consensus cracks, a democratic polity is unable to deal with a challenge like Tibet. Then everything must revert from the means of democratic processes back to the bases of the liberal principle, from which a search for a new system will begin.

I believe that this liberal principle is a necessary condition for solving the Tibetan issue. Only based on this principle can individual self-determination gain legitimacy. Only in this way can collective self-determination from "others," and the discussions of definitions of collectivities, such as Tibetan people, Tibetan nation, Chinese, Chinese nation, and so on, find a rational beginning.

In light of the fact that Tibetans, both within the PRC borders and in exile, are highly aware of their distinctiveness from the Chinese, their group rights have to be addressed in some form relative to the group rights of Chinese (even though, with the liberal principle elaborated earlier, concepts such as group rights or any other collectivistic notion become theoretically groundless). At the same time, Chinese have no more legitimacy in claiming such group rights than Tibetans. Here reciprocity is fair, and fairness becomes justice. But turning from what is immediately fair to search for what is possible and what is best, we must discuss the logical possibilities for a relationship between an ethnic majority and a minority such as Chinese and Tibetans. These are discussed below.

## Assimilation

So far, most, if not all, Tibetans have expressed a strong distaste for assimilation. At the same time, without governmental or fanatical propaganda, I doubt that there will be many Chinese who favor Tibetan assimilation, in the absence of any grounded reasoning demonstrating a benefit to the Chinese. Even if such reasoning is provided and corroborated, there is much to be said for not having a repressed group of people within the control of China.

## Separation

A desire for separation or independence for Tibet is voiced loudly and clearly by the Tibetan elite. But even if we put aside the current political pressure from Beijing and other geopolitical complications,[9] the issues of territorial boundaries and, most important, of the right of non-Tibetans within the area who will become new minorities[10] may well make the road for independence a tortuous one, even a dead end. Independence cannot be established at the cost of loss of freedom for non-Tibetans in Tibet. Too often, history has recorded the irony of the oppressed being freed from their yoke and then becoming oppressive. Freedom from former oppressors is often followed by freedom to enchain the newfound slaves. Hatred among all three main ethnic groups—Tibetans, Han Chinese, and Hui in the Tibet region, long suppressed—could fuel endless conflicts soon after the iron hands of communist repression are gone.

The problems of these possibilities oblige us to find better solutions. Searching through history one sees that not every ethnicity has found its political expression in the form of nation-state. There are far more ethnicities than there are nation-states. Although many general as well as specific reasons outside the control of ethnic groups have prevented nationalist movements from forming or succeeding,[11] there are also cases where the ethnic group chose to stay within the multinational state.[12] These cases provide another logical possibility: integration.

## *Integration*

What integration implies is first an understanding of the modern polity. Modern polity—left or right—presumes a nation-state based on some form of a politically motivated citizenry. If the road of political participation is open for every citizen within the country, and if the power center can select its members by means accepted by all groups in the country, such an entity—such as liberal democracy—can contribute to the formation of a kind of national consciousness that could define common traits of the citizenry beyond the conventional ethnic concepts or other cultural and religious formulations.

The integration principle also implies a consistency with the liberal principle as indicated earlier. Everyone is included, not by their membership in an ethnic group, or for that matter wealth, intelligence, physical strength, or gender, but by virtue of being a citizen in a participatory, open society.

Integration as a solution to ethnic problems such as those in Tibet can provide a logical alternative to assimilation and separation. But from the perspective of elite politics, if a new elite, or an old one that lost its influence, finds the open political system not open enough to fulfill its will for power and influence, ethnic nationalism will be one of the easiest weapons it can use. And the contents of such an ethnic nationalism can be formulated in a way that will give a uniqueness to the group the elite claims to represent and therefore enable it to incite that group for the needed mobilization of mass support. Such ethnic nationalism can provide the strength for staging a serious confrontation with the establishment. So even if the current repression in China ends with a new, truly democratic governance that genuinely views every citizen politically equal in the formal sense (the legal sense, for example), the new elevation of Tibetans through their newly acquired political rights may fall short of their desire to find collective political expression in their own nation-state.

Again, from the angle of individual rights, all these formulations have to be contested before the individuals whose choice should serve as the final verdict.

It is impossible to predict the success of the integration principle in the Tibet situation. It is a rational choice, pitted against irrational forces and provoked by appeals to ethnic nationalism. But I remain hopeful for such a solution on two grounds: the validity of the idea itself and the current attitude of the Tibetan exile leadership.

In my numerous meetings since 1989 with His Holiness the Dalai Lama, he has repeatedly expressed his view that independence is not and should not be the primary goal of his movement. As long as genuine autonomy of the Tibetans can be respected and their basic human rights guaranteed, he sees no reason not to remain in touch with the Chinese. Issues of polity and sovereignty aside, a clear understanding came out of these meetings. Peaceful coexistence and mutually beneficial development should be the real substance of a Chinese–Tibetan relationship. The Dalai Lama's political view is not completely representative of all Tibetans, but it does have a large following. In view of his absolute religious authority in Tibetan Buddhism, Tibetans in and outside Tibet and their Western supporters are obliged to make a serious attempt to remain open-minded as to the form of Tibet's political future.

This article attempts only to lay out some very basic concepts and principles for dealing with the Tibetan issue and seeking an answer. As indicated earlier, the wisdom, practicality, and tactics of the Chinese and Tibetan people will be pivotal to the ultimate solution of this issue. Thus the establishment of a principle alone cannot offer a concrete solution. I am convinced, though, that the belief in such a fundamental principle—a liberal principle—is a precondition of any meaningful attempt to solve the problem.

In the wilderness of the Tibetan issue and others like it, our belief in freedom, our wisdom, and our courage will print hope on the future pages of our history. A Chinese writer once talked about hope: Hope is like a path in the wilderness, he said; there is no road in the beginning, but after brave people repeatedly walk down the path, one is formed. This hope will open up a new world, and this path will lead us to a new horizon where every Chinese and every Tibetan will live side by side, whatever the polity, peacefully, not as members of mutually exclusive races but as brothers and sisters, as members of the human race, each with dignity. I call on the Chinese to wake up and, in the light of the dawn of liberalism, reexamine the unavoidable Tibetan issue.

## Notes

1. Several factors have played an important role in the Chinese psyche—chauvinist prejudice, the assumed prerequisite of "Chinese Han" nationalism, and the Chinese people's own feelings of insecurity as a result of their having been more or less the underclass in modern history.

2. This more fundamental value is the sublime and uncompromising esteem of negative freedom—a formulation coined by Isaiah Berlin—which is the "freedom from" as compared to the "freedom to." See Section IV of this article.

3. If *national* means a congruence between political and cultural boundaries (not ethnic, even though the "cultural" is often portrayed as "ethnic"), then nationalism is a basic style of thinking and an organizing principle of modern polity. Democracy—one of the most salient and cherished forms of a modern entity—presumes nationalism. In my modernist line of understanding nationalism, the ethnic is seen only as a cultural construction. Empirically the ethnicity on which modern nation-states are based comprises cultural and symbolic inventions and imaginations. Nations in the sense of nation-states are

conceived not from within the traditions and collective memories of the "national" groups that carry them, but from without; that is, a historic contingency becomes widespread, and elements of tradition and ethnicity are present only to the extent that they are utilized to fill the skeleton of the national idea with flesh and blood.

4. It could be argued that the peaceful coexistence of the ethnicity in these nation-states is the result of a certain kind of formulation of nationality that has taken roots in the social consciousness. This formulation manages to include all these groups in the family of citizenship, and elevates, at least in theory, the previously marginalized and repressed social groups or ethnicity to a level equal to the other privileged groups. Such formulation then takes effect through literature, art, national monuments, census, maps, natural and historical sites, and standardized education.

5. In the northwestern region, there is an independence movement of eastern Turkistan; some in Inner Mongolia never withdrew their claim of a certain form of independence, be it with Mongolia or as an independent Southern Mongolia. Unique historical paths also put Hong Kong, Macao, and Taiwan into the consideration for alternative forms of polity—not the empire-style management by China that the Communists have been demanding for the past half-century.

6. The issue of Tibetan sovereignty is a new problem in the context of modern history, rather than ancient history.

7. That is, other influential modern political ideas and philosophies.

8. It is therefore sometimes referred to as "the second best" or "the necessary evil."

9. For example, the Sino-Indian relationship.

10. Other than Chinese immigrants who went to Tibet at different historical periods (not all under the Chinese Communist regime's program of immigration), a significant portion of the population in Tibet is Hui (Muslim).

11. For example, lack of high culture that will inspire or respond to the call of nationalism, an extremely small population, external naked oppressive power, and so on.

12. For example, the American civil rights movement in the 1960s, modern Scottish unionism in Great Britain, even the difficult Quebec issue in Canada, and so on.

# Reflections on the Seventeen-point Agreement of 1951

## Song Liming

In the modern history of Tibet, nothing has been more important than the Seventeen-point Agreement of 1951.[1] It is the only formal Sino-Tibetan treaty since the treaty of 821. There is, however, a distinct difference between these two agreements. The treaty of 821 was concluded at a time when Tibet was powerful and independent. It called for Tibet and China to abide by the acknowledged frontiers. "All to the east is the country of Great China; all to the west is the country of Great Tibet."[2] By contrast, the Seventeen-point Agreement declared that Tibet had become part of China, providing as it did that "the Tibetan people shall return to the big family of the Motherland—the People's Republic of China" (Point 1); the Tibetan government should actively assist the People's Liberation Army (PLA) to enter Tibet and consolidate their national defenses (Point 2); Tibetan troops should be reorganized step by step into the Chinese army (Point 8); and China should be responsible for all of Tibet's external affairs (Point 14). However, the same agreement promised that the Tibetan people would have the right to exercise autonomy in their ethnic region (Point 3); the Chinese government would not alter the existing political system in Tibet or the established status, functions, and powers of the Dalai Lama and the Panchen Lama (Points 4, 5); the religious beliefs, costumes, and habits of the Tibetan people would be respected and lamaseries would be protected (Point 7); and internal reforms would take place only after consultations with Tibetan leaders and without compulsion by China (Point 11).

The Seventeen-point Agreement is far from perfect. The lengthy preamble is typical, often illogical, communist propaganda. It states that the people of Tibet were being liberated from external and internal enemies—foreign imperialist and the Chinese Nationalist forces. This makes little sense. It is well known that, on the eve of the Chinese army's attack on Tibet, hardly any foreigners were in Tibet, and there were no Chinese Nationalists at all. Moreover, there has been no divergence between the Chinese Communists' and Nationalists' policies toward Tibet. Take, for example, the Sino-Tibetan negotiations in 1934, when General Huang Musong (the Nationalists' deputy chief of the General Staff) put forward the following proposal as the basis of a Sino-Tibetan agreement: While the Tibetan political system would be preserved and Tibetan autonomy granted, Tibet must be an integral part of China and the Chinese central government would be responsible for diplomacy, national defense, communications, and the appointment of high officials in Tibet.[3] It looks almost as though this proposal laid down the foundations for the Seventeen-point Agreement. In fact the only opponent of the Chinese Communists in Tibet was none other than the Tibetan government, which for years had maintained the country's independence and refused to be "liberated peacefully" before its troops were actually routed. It all had precious little to do with the foreign imperialists and nothing at all to do with the Chinese Nationalists.

The text of the Seventeen-point Agreement has other defects. It is said that, during the 1951 negotiations in Beijing, disagreement arose over various points. For example, on discussing Point 15 ("In order to ensure the implementation of this Agreement, the central people's government shall set up a military and administrative committee and a military area headquarters in Tibet") the Tibetans argued that it conflicted with Point 4, that the central government would not alter the existing political system in Tibet. However, when the irritated Chinese threatened to renew military attack, the Tibetans decided they had to acquiesce. It may be added that Point 6 seems inconsistent with China's policy that Beijing should maintain control over Tibet, while at the same time the Dalai Lama and the Panchen Lama had some ill-defined authority. But it seems to me that these particular defects could have been resolved if the real purpose of the Seventeen-point Agreement was to maintain Tibet's autonomy under China's sovereignty in the same way that the purpose of the Simla Convention of 1914 was to maintain Tibet's autonomy under China's suzerainty.[4]

A more serious question concerns the legality of the Seventeen-point Agreement. One popular view holds that "because it was signed under duress, the Agreement lacked validity under international law."[5] That the Agreement was signed under duress is self-evident, since the Tibetan government was coerced into accepting the agreement after troops in Kham suffered defeat and were in no position to resist the advance of the Chinese troops. However, that the agreement lacked validity under international law for this reason is questionable. As some leading jurists have pointed out: "The law on the effect of duress on treaties is ... subject to conflicting opinions, and no useful purpose would be served by preferring one to the other."[6] As with most peace treaties, the Seventeen-point Agreement resulted from a war. If one prefers to think that treaties signed under duress are illegal, one should use the same standard to judge the Seventeen-point Agreement and other similar treaties—for example, the treaty between Tibet and Nepal of 1856 and the convention between Great Britain and Tibet of 1904, both of which were undoubtedly imposed on the Tibetans by others. It seems, though, that a double standard has been in effect here: on the one hand, the Seventeen-point Agreement is seen as illegal; on the other hand, the treaties that Tibet concluded with the Nepalese and the British, respectively, under the same or similar circumstance are viewed as legal and even are used as evidence of Tibet's international personality and independence. By the same standard, one has to say that all three treaties are either equally legal or equally illegal. Thus Tibet either lost its independence by the Seventeen-point Agreement even though it had been a full independent state in the past, or Tibet lacked the evidence of independence, at least during the Qing dynasty.

In fact scholars generally agree that Tibet was not a fully independent state during the Qing dynasty but was such only after 1912.[7] Tibet's status vis-à-vis China has not been immutable and frozen; instead, it has been capricious and changeable. If 1951 saw a turning point in the history of Sino-Tibetan relations, 1912 had seen another one. With the outbreak of the Chinese Revolution of 1911 and the collapse of the Manchu Empire, the Chinese troops in Tibet were divided into two parts, one pro-emperor, the other pro-republicans. They fought against each other, and the Tibetans fought against them both, in the end successfully. By 1912, when the Thirteenth Dalai Lama returned from exile in India and ordered the expulsion of all Chinese, Tibet was free of Chinese control. There is no doubt that the changes in both 1912 and 1951 were accompanied by violence. The Tibetan government was reluctant to accept what happened in 1951, just as the Chinese government after 1912 had refused to recognize the fait accompli. The difference between the two is that the change in 1951 was a Sino-Tibetan agreement whereas in 1912 there was no real agreement (although the abortive Simla Conference tried to convince the Chinese to make an agreement with the Tibetans as well as with the British). Thus the question is this: Was there a legal basis for Tibet's independence after 1912?

To this question there is one ready answer. Apparently [the British official Charles] Bell argued for the first time that the connection between China and Tibet originated with the Manchu dynasty, [based on mutual devotion to] Buddhism, and that logically the relationship came to an end with the extinction of that dynasty.[8] This view has often been repeated. But when Bell made this pronouncement in 1946, he could not have foreseen an uncomfortable parallel, that of the transfer of power in India, which began in 1947, in which the Indians became the masters of an independent India in place of the British. Following Bell's reasoning, one might say: "Inasmuch as the connection between India and Tibet was originated by the British Empire, it logically came to an end with the disappearance of the British from India." But insufficient attention has been paid to such a parallel. The following is another example of the double standard. By that standard, the Republic of China could inherit the Qing dynasty's rights in Tibet as the Republic of India had. Since the Republic of India had inherited British rights in Tibet without any problem, it is difficult to deny the similar claims of the Republic of China. Thus the legal basis for the independence of Tibet from 1912 to 1951 remained open to question.[9]

The Seventeen-point Agreement is embarrassing not only to those who maintain that Tibet has been an independent state but for those who hold that Tibet has always been part of China. If China had had sovereignty over Tibet before 1951, why did China need to conclude the Seventeen-point Agreement? No treaty or agreement should have been necessary had Tibet already been part of China. Some Chinese officials, both during the Qing dynasty and the Chinese Republic, thought this way. Here are two examples: On the eve of the Chinese army's entry into Lhasa in 1910, the Vice Amban Wen Zongyao wanted to make an agreement with the Thirteenth Dalai Lama; the Amban Lian Yu did not agree with him, however, arguing that Tibet was a dependent state of China and so no treaty need be concluded between them.[10] In 1944 Shen Ts'ung-lien (Shen Conglian), the Chinese representative in Tibet, told the British that since Tibet was part of China, any settlement by means of a Sino-Tibetan treaty was out of the question. It would be superfluous and absurd for one part of a country to enter into international treaties with another part of the same country.[11] Of course this makes sense.

Accordingly, the Seventeen-point Agreement has posed a paradox for the Chinese government: If it regards the Agreement as an accomplishment, it has to recognize that Tibet had not been part of China before 1951; if it insists that China has always had sovereignty over Tibet, then it has to admit that making an agreement was silly. Logically, it needed to make a choice, but in fact it seems to have been impossible for it to do so. It does not think it was a blunder to have made the Seventeen-point Agreement, and that is a reasonable view. But on the other hand, it cannot bring itself to admit that Tibet had been a separate entity, otherwise what it had done in 1950 is not the liberation of Tibet, as it proudly declared, but rather the occupation of a nation, as most Western scholars see it. The Chinese Communists have called themselves the emancipators of the Chinese in general, the liberators of the Tibetans in particular. By making such extravagant claims, they erected a hurdle too high for them to clear. As a result, what they try to do is to eat their cake and have it too; they insist that before 1950 Tibet had been part of China, while greatly esteeming the Seventeen-point Agreement and even celebrating the making of it on occasion.

Although the Chinese government is reluctant to make the choice, the Seventeen-point Agreement actually makes it for them. Apart from the fact that China did conclude it, it is worth noting that in the agreement the Tibetan representatives were called plenipotentiaries, a title usually not given to delegates of a so-called local government. Moreover, Point 1 provided that "the Tibetan people shall return to the big family of the Motherland," which implies that in the past Tibet had been out of the "big family of the Motherland." Point 8 stipulated that "Tibetan troops shall be reorganized step by step into the PLA and become a part of the national defense of the PRC," which acknowledges that Tibet, in the past, had had its own troops and that China had not been responsible for Tibet's national defense. Point 14 specified that "The PRC shall have centralized handling of all external affairs of the area of Tibet," which correctly implies that Tibet had previously conducted its own diplomatic affairs. History cannot be falsified; all the articles in the Seventeen-point Agreement that established Chinese sovereignty over Tibet simply reveal the preexisting reality: Before 1951 China had not controlled Tibet's diplomacy and national defense and therefore had no sovereignty over Tibet. In fact most Western scholars agree that from 1912 to

1951 Tibet had been at least de facto independent, a view, to some degree, shared even by a few Chinese scholars.[12]

Since the Seventeen-point Agreement ended Tibet's independence, it was certainly a loss for the Tibetan government; but having maintained significant autonomy, the agreement in and of itself did not mean that they had lost everything. After Tibetan troops in Kham were routed, after hopes were dashed that neighboring countries could aid them, and after appeals to the United Nations went unheeded, the Tibetan government had few options. When news of the agreement's conclusion was announced, Tibetan leaders in Dromo (Yadong) [on the Indian border] had two choices: accept the agreement or reject it and seek asylum in India. After long and heated debate, the National Assembly decided that the agreement could be accepted because it did not threaten the status and power of the Dalai Lama; nor did it endanger the traditional Tibetan religious and political system.

The Dalai Lama explained in 1959: "We were obliged to acquiesce and decided to abide by the terms and conditions in order to save our people and country from total destruction." But eight years after accepting the agreement, the Dalai Lama and his government finally decided to leave Lhasa and seek asylum in India—precisely because Tibetan autonomy was dying.

What the Tibetans lost in the agreement the Chinese gained, although the Chinese did not get all that they desired. By means of the Seventeen-point Agreement, they forced the Tibetans to acknowledge, for the first time in history, China's sovereignty, so it was a great victory for them, enabling them to make their predecessors' dreams a reality. On the other hand, Tibet was promised a high degree of autonomy. For a dictator like Mao Zedong, this could not have been granted lightly. Actually, subsequent events revealed that the Chinese government was not satisfied with Tibet having autonomy; eventually Lhasa would have to be forced to make further concessions. But this would have to wait. As a newly established regime, apart from many internal difficulties, the Chinese government was preparing to "liberate" Taiwan, which was occupied by the Chinese Nationalists, and engaged in the Korean War against UN troops. Under such circumstances, the Chinese government urgently needed to resolve the Tibetan problem. The Seventeen-point Agreement, therefore, is a compromise between the Chinese and Tibetan governments. This formula ostensibly allowed Tibet to have its own system, within the framework of the Chinese People's Republic.

As mentioned above, Point 4 of the agreement stipulated that the Chinese government should not change the existing political system in Tibet. What was this political system? In the view of some, it was feudal serfdom; for others it was a dual religious-political system. In any case, it was different from the political system in China. This means that, in effect, the Seventeen-point Agreement embodied a formula of "one country, two systems."[13] This fact, however, has been generally ignored; most people believe that the formula of "one country, two systems" was invented by Deng Xiaoping for the settlement of the future of Hong Kong and Taiwan. This erroneous impression is shared even by the writers of the Seventeen-point Agreement. For example, in the 1982 Sino-Tibetan exploratory talks, the Tibetans requested that the "one nation, two systems" formula that Beijing had promised to Taiwan should be extended to Tibet because Tibet's unique historical status and special characteristics surely warranted special treatment. The Chinese rejected this on the grounds that Tibet's case was different since Sino-Tibetan relations had already been determined by the Seventeen-point Agreement and "Tibetans should not turn back the wheels of history." But the Tibetans retorted that they had been compelled to repudiate the agreement because it was signed "under duress" and because the Chinese authorities in Tibet had betrayed it.[14]

In any case, the Seventeen-point Agreement was short-lived. It died in 1959 when a Tibetan popular revolt against Chinese rule was suppressed and the Dalai Lama and his followers fled to India. From then on, the Tibetan government-in-exile repudiated the Seventeen-point Agreement as invalid. Although the Chinese government still claims that the agreement is legal, the Tibetan government[-in-exile] says that the Chinese government violated every undertaking in it and insists it was the Chinese who were responsible for the outbreak of the 1959 conflict and therefore the death of the agreement. On the other hand, the Chinese government charges that the Tibetans "deliberately violated and sabotaged the Seventeen-point Agreement and intensified their efforts to split the motherland."[15]

Thus the responsibility for the death of the agreement has also become a subject of dispute. Evidence indicates that the Chinese government failed to fulfill the obligations under the agreement. For example, in parts of Tibet they immediately began altering the existing political system by imposing the so-called democratic reforms, and soon they eroded the authority of the Dalai Lama in many ways. It is not quite accurate, however, to say that the Chinese government betrayed every clause of the agreement. It respected the clauses relating to China's sovereignty over Tibet. What it failed to honor were the clauses concerning Tibet's autonomy. On the other hand, just as the Chinese disliked "two systems," the Tibetans disliked "one country." They originally tried to impede the entry of Chinese troops into Tibet; since then, they have advocated Tibetan independence. The Sino-Tibetan conflicts, especially the revolt of 1959, were not only a reaction to Chinese violation of the Agreement but were also a protest against the agreement itself or an attempt to expel the Chinese from Tibet and to regain Tibetan independence. Thus it would be fair to say that regardless of the agreement between the Chinese and Tibetans, it led to the conflict of 1959 and eventually to the agreement's demise. At most, one can argue that the Chinese bear more responsibility than the Tibetans.

The 1959 revolt is a watershed in the modern history of Sino-Tibetan relations. As Tibet lost its independence in 1951 by the signing of the Seventeen-point Agreement, it lost its autonomy in 1959 with the death of the agreement. Because of the flight of the Dalai Lama and his followers to India, there was a power vacuum in Tibet; the Chinese government then took the opportunity not only to fill the void but to institute the so-called democratic reforms. These "reforms" had already been completed in Inner

Tibet; now they were to be implemented in Tibet proper as well, supposedly to advance Tibet from "the hell of feudalism" to a "socialist paradise." Thus "one country, two systems" became "one country, one system," and Tibetan autonomy from then on would be merely nominal. Undoubtedly it was the Chinese government that gave the coup de grâce to the Seventeen-point Agreement; all the Tibetan government did was to announce the news of its death publicly. Thus it is ironic that, as occurred in the 1982 Sino-Tibetan talks, the Tibetans viewed the agreement as a vulgarity, while the Chinese cited it eagerly.

The death of the Seventeen-point Agreement has been devastating for the Tibetans. In the 1959 conflict and the subsequent political movements, especially during the Cultural Revolution, thousands of Tibetans were killed,[16] arrested, or taken to concentration camps. Tibetan cultural and religious institutions were destroyed.[17] Oddly enough, the death of the agreement did not advance Chinese interests at all. Internally, the Tibetans are unhappy with direct Chinese rule, and the situation in Tibet has been tense. Externally, since 1959, China's Tibetan policy has been condemned by the international community, which had been silent when Tibet lost its independence in 1951. In short, the death of the agreement did not resolve the Tibetan issue; instead the issue has become more serious and more international. Accordingly, both the Chinese and the Tibetans in exile find it necessary to change the situation. Under these circumstances, at the very beginning of the post-Mao era, Sino-Tibetan negotiations resumed.[18]

The long Sino-Tibetan dialogues have yielded no results. In theory, there is plenty of room for agreement. The Tibetan government, except for a short period, has requested only Tibet's autonomy or the formula of "one country, two systems," as indicated in the recent talks of the Dalai Lama. The Chinese government has been insistent only on Chinese sovereignty over Tibet; the Chinese leaders, including Deng Xiaoping, have repeated that China is willing to discuss and resolve with the Tibetans all issues short of the independence of Tibet. In this sense, it should not be difficult to find a basis for Sino-Tibetan negotiations. In practice, though, no mutually acceptable basis for negotiations has been found. In 1981 the then general secretary of the CCP, Hu Yaobang, put forward the "Five-point Proposal to the Dalai Lama."[19] The Dalai Lama rejected it firmly by remarking, "Instead of addressing the real issues facing the six million Tibetan people, China has attempted to reduce the question of Tibet to a discussion of my own personal status." In 1988 the Dalai Lama issued the Strasbourg Proposal as the "framework for Sino-Tibetan negotiations."[20] The Chinese government refused it by arguing that "China's sovereignty over Tibet brooks no denial. Of Tibet there can be no independence, no semi-independence, no independence in disguise."

If we analyze these two proposals on the basis of the Seventeen-point Agreement, it is easy to see why the Tibetans feel that the Chinese government is not offering them very much. More precisely, the Chinese government is unwilling to give Tibet a high degree of autonomy, even that which was embodied in the Seventeen-point agreement, and now the Tibetan government is unwilling to recognize China's full sovereignty, which was specified in the Agreement. By comparison, however, the Dalai Lama's proposal is closer to the agreement than was Hu Yaobang's—even though it was the Tibetan government that repudiated the agreement in 1959, while the Chinese government still regards it as legal. This strange phenomenon, coupled with the bizarre episode in the 1982 exploratory talks, suggests that the makers of the Seventeen-point Agreement have forgotten everything about their product except its name. That explains why both the Chinese and Tibetans were so confused during the 1982 exploratory talks; in order to demand the formula of "one country, two systems," the Tibetans should have simply based their request on the agreement rather than on Beijing's promise to Taiwan; in order to refuse it, the Chinese should have avoided any mention of the agreement. One can speculate as to what, if the Tibetans and Chinese had argued along opposite lines, the result would have been. In a broader sense, had the Tibetan government accepted the agreement, should the Chinese government have been amenable? Or if the Chinese government had made the same proposal, should the Tibetan government have been so angry? In short, can the Seventeen-point Agreement serve as a basis for a new Sino-Tibetan historical compromise?

To return to the Seventeen-point Agreement might cause the Tibetan government to lose face, since it publicly repudiated it in 1959. In politics, however, face should always be a secondary consideration. If Tibetan independence is the goal, then repudiation of the agreement is important; otherwise "independence" would be meaningless. If the government is willing to settle for less, it can find the fundamental elements in the Seventeen-point Agreement, such as the formula of "one country, two systems." And it cannot expect to achieve other gains through negotiations with the Chinese. The Tibetan government should realize that in 1951, when it accepted the agreement, it lost Tibet's independence. If it should return to it now, at least Tibet would regain its autonomy. If the original motive for accepting the agreement was to avoid Tibet's total destruction, to return to it now would serve the same purpose. More important, if the government requested real Tibetan autonomy, or "one country, two systems" on the basis of the Seventeen-point Agreement, the Chinese government would have difficulty refusing it. It is also worth noting that to return to the Seventeen-point Agreement would not necessarily mean restoring the traditional Tibetan political system, because, as indicated in the Strasbourg Proposal, the agreement provided that the Tibetan people, together with their leaders, would determine the nature of any new political system there.[21] Besides, if the Tibetan government were to make clear that all it wants is "one country, two systems," it would win more sympathy and support among the Chinese, especially those in Taiwan and Hong Kong, who so far have paid little attention to the Tibetan cause [but for whom the issue of "one country, two systems" has much relevance].

One would expect the Chinese government to be more reluctant than the Tibetans to return to the Seventeen-point Agreement because by doing so it would be ceding substantial authority that it has enjoyed in Tibet. But since the government still regards the agreement as legal, how can it refuse to do so? Real autonomy, or the formula of "one country, two systems," would not contradict its claim of sovereignty over Tibet, so it cannot interpret it as "turning back the wheels of history" or "independence in disguise," as was its reaction to Tibetan's request in 1982 and to the Strasbourg Proposal. The government should realize that direct Chinese rule in Tibet after 1959 has proved to be a failure, and only real autonomy for Tibet can save the country from trouble both domestically and internationally. Moreover, to settle the Tibetan issue in this way would send a positive signal to Hong Kong and Taiwan. Currently, the Chinese government is eager to show good faith in the formula of "one country, two systems" to Hong Kong and Taiwan, but why should the people of Hong Kong and Taiwan trust the Chinese? China is undoubtedly responsible for the violation of the Seventeen-point Agreement and thus for the termination of Tibet's "existing political system." In order to prove its good faith with respect to the "one country, two systems" promise to Hong Kong and Taiwan, Beijing, first of all, should acknowledge its past errors in the treatment of Tibet and grant Tibet its own political system and autonomy.

In consideration of Tibet's actual situation, there is an urgent necessity for the Chinese and Tibetan governments to resolve the Tibetan issue through peaceful and reasonable negotiations as soon as possible. I believe that to return to the Seventeen-point Agreement would be the most feasible, though perhaps not ideal, solution.

## Notes

1. *Agreement of the Central People's Government and the Local Government of Tibet on Measures for the Peaceful Liberation of Tibet* was concluded in Beijing by Chinese and Tibetan plenipotentiaries on May 23, 1951. It includes a preamble and a text of seventeen points, so it is commonly known as the Seventeen-point Agreement. It is said that three separate (secret) clauses exist dealing with the Tibetan army and police, the future of the Dalai Lama,

and Tibetan currency. See Melvyn Goldstein, *A History of Modern Tibet, 1913–1951: The Demise of the Lamaist State* (Berkeley: University of California Press, 1991), p. 770; and Tsering Shakya, "The Genesis of the Sino-Tibetan Agreement of 1951," in *Tibetan Studies, Proceedings of the Sixth Seminar of the International Association for Tibetan Studies* (Oslo: n.p., 1994).

2. For an English translation of the Treaty of 821 as well as that of the Seventeen-point Agreement, see Hugh Richardson, *Tibet and Its History* (Boulder and London: Shambala, 1984), appendix.

3. *Selected Files Relating to the Memorial Ceremony on the Demise of the Thirteenth Dalai Lama and the Reincarnation and Installation of the Fourteenth Dalai Lama* (Shisan shi dalai yuanji zhiji he shisi shi dalai zhuanshi zuochuang dang'an xuanbian) (Beijing: Chinese Center for Tibetology and the Second Historical Archives, 1990), pp. 106–107.

4. For the best analyses of the Simla Convention see Alastair Lamb, *Tibet, China, and India 1914–1950, A History of Imperial Diplomacy* (Hertingfordbury, UK: Roxford Books, 1989), pp. 12–15.

5. Michael van Walt van Praag, "Introduction" to *The Legal Status of Tibet, Three Studies by Leading Jurists* (Dharamsala: Office of Information and International Relations, 1989).

6. "The Status of Tibet," in *Tibet and the Chinese People's Republic, A Report to the International Commission of Jurists by Its Legal Inquiry Committee on Tibet* (Geneva: International Commission of Jurists, 1960), p. 164.

7. The Sino-Tibetan relationship in the Qing dynasty has been generally interpreted by most Western scholars as that of protectorate or suzerainty, although by Tibetan and Chinese scholars, respectively, as that of Cho-yon (patron and priest) and sovereignty. See T. W. Shakabpa, *Tibet: A Political History* (New Haven and London: Yale University Press, 1967) and Li Tieh-tseng, *The Historical Status of Tibet* (New York: King's Crown Press, 1956).

8. Charles Bell, *Portrait of a Dalai Lama, the Life and Times of the Great Thirteenth* (London: Wisdom, 1987), p. 329.

9. Of course the similar question should be asked: "What is the legal basis for the Manchu's rule in Tibet?" It is not easy to make a legal judgment as to what happened historically. In any case, students of history may limit themselves to studying what happened, and if possible, why it happened.

10. *Memorials to the Emperor by Amban Lian Yu* (Lian Yu zhu Zang chaodu), ed. Wu Fengpei (Lhasa: Renmin chubanshe, 1979), p. 110.

11. L/PS/12/4217, Viceroy to Secretary of State, October, 1944. Lamb, p. 331.

12. For example, Shen and Liu remark: "Since 1911 Lhasa has to all practical purposes enjoyed full independence"; see Shen Tsung-lian and Liu Sheng-chi, *Tibet and the Tibetans* (Stanford: Stanford University Press, 1953; repr. New York, 1973), p. 62. Yang points out: "Before Liberation a situation of de facto semi-independence existed in Tibet." See Yang Gongsu, *A History of China's Struggle against Foreign Invasion and Interference in Tibet* (Zhongguo fandui waiguo jinlue ganshe Xizang difang douzheng shi) (Beijing: Zhongguo Zangxue chubanshe, 1992), p. 246.

13. Jiang Ping, former vice director of the Department of the United Front and now vice director of China's Center of Tibetology, remarks that 1959 saw "the termination of the phase of coexistence of two political powers." See Jiang Ping and others, *The Tibetan Nationality's Regional Autonomy* (Xizang de minzu quyup zizhi) (Beijing: n.p., 1991), p. 55. The term *coexistence* is also used by Goldstein. See Melvyn Goldstein, "The Dragon and the Snow Lion: the Tibetan Question in the Twentieth Century," *Tibetan Review* (April 1991): 12.

14. Dawa Norbu, "China's Dialogue with the Dalai Lama 1978–90: Prenegotiation Stage or Dead End?" *Tibetan Review* (May 1992): 13, 16.

15. *Tibet—Its Ownership and Human Rights Situation* (Beijing: Information Office of the State Council of the PRC, 1992), p. 22.

16. According to the Tibetan government, "More than 1.2 million Tibetans have died as a direct result of the Chinese invasion and occupation of Tibet." See *Tibet: Proving Truth from Facts* (Dharamsala: Department of Information and International Relations, 1994).

17. Some believe that if the Agreement had remained intact, such a catastrophe might have been avoided. See Ngapo Ngawang Jigme, "The True Facts of the 10 March 1959 Event," *China Tibetology* [Beijing], no. 2 (1988): 5.

18. It is also said that the Chinese and Tibetans had been in contact since as far back as the early 1970s. See Tsering Wangyal, "Sino-Tibetan Negotiations Since 1959," in *Resistance and Reform in Tibet,* ed. Robert Barnett and Shirin Akiner (London: Hurst, 1994), p. 197.

19. It is stated in Hu's proposal that the Dalai Lama and his entourage are welcome to return and settle in China, and that if and when he returns, his political and economic privileges shall be as they were before 1959; he will be appointed vice president of the National People's Congress as well as vice chairman of the Chinese People's Political Consultative Conference. It is said that the condition that the Dalai Lama had to reside in Beijing was withdrawn in 1986. See Dawa Norbu, "China's Dialogue with the Dalai Lama," p. 16.

20. It is stated in the Strasbourg Proposal that China can remain responsible for Tibet's foreign policy; meanwhile, Tibet should have its own Foreign Affairs Bureau to deal with commerce, education, religion, and other nonpolitical activities; as to defense, China can have the right to maintain a restricted number of military installations in Tibet until such time as demilitarization and neutralization can be achieved through a regional peace conference and international agreement; it is also demanded that all of Greater Tibet, known as Cholkha-sum, should become "a self-governing, democratic political entity founded on law by agreement of the people . . . in association with the People's Republic of China." See *Government Resolutions and International Documents on Tibet* (Dharamsala: Office of Information and International Relations, 1989), pp. 11–15.

21. It is stated in the Seventeen-point Agreement that: "[i]n matters related to various reforms in Tibet, there will be no compulsion on the part of the central government. The local government of Tibet should carry out reforms of its own accord, and when the people raise demands for reform, they shall be

settled by means of consultation with the leading personnel of Tibet" (Point 11). In the Strasbourg Proposal it is stated that "whatever the outcome of the negotiations with the Chinese may be, the Tibetan people must be the ultimate deciding authority. Therefore any proposal will contain a comprehensive procedural plan in a nationwide referendum to ascertain the wishes of the Tibetan people."

# The Status of Tibet: Recalling a Visit to Lhasa

## Wang Ruowang

In 1982 I had a chance to visit Tibet with a group organized by the Chinese Writers and Artists Association. While learning a lot about Tibetan culture, history, and customs in Tibet, we were also strongly impressed by the suffering that the Chinese Communist government had inflicted on the Tibetan people.

During the period that China practiced the "people's commune" system in the countryside, Tibet was also forced by the Chinese Communist government to follow the Maoist pattern; the government compelled the Tibetans to form communes. They confiscated Tibetans' private livestock for collective animal husbandry and also practiced collective farming as well as collective leadership. Gradually almost all the livestock of the "people's communes" died and, soon thereafter, about 300,000 Tibetans starved to death. This was the year after the worst starvation in China, which had been caused by Mao's Great Leap Forward. Comparing the mortality rate with the six million people of Tibet, we find that 5 percent of Tibetans died of starvation, whereas the death rate in China was 2.7 percent.

The Tibetan's greatest indignation arose from the fact that during the Cultural Revolution the People's Liberation Army and the Red Guards destroyed almost all the temples in Tibet. This was followed by China proper's movement to "eliminate the four olds" (old ideas, old culture, old costumes, and old habits). Unlike the situation in China proper, the Tibetans were so poor that they had little property for the Red Guards to loot or destroy, so the Red Guards destroyed the Tibetan temples instead. According to the political analyst of the International Campaign for Tibet, Jigme Ngapo, the son of the former vice chairman of the Chinese National People's Congress, "The most painful thing the Tibetan people endured was the demolition of their temples. The Tibetans had spent more than half their money on building temples and providing oil for the lights in the temples, while enduring poverty themselves."

When confronted with the destroyed temples, members of our group were all distressed. A former Tibetan lama, who had been forced to resume secular life, told us this story: A Chinese named Jin from Sichuan was sent to Tibet to head a county. During the Cultural Revolution, he stirred up open rebellion against the Tibetans, especially the Buddhist monks and their temples. He made a fortune by collecting all sorts of gold-plated Buddha statues, and he even commandeered the Tibetans' horses to carry the booty to his home in Sichuan. The lama sadly told us: "I am a monk, I do not want to lead a secular life; I am afraid Buddha will punish me. But with our monasteries all destroyed, where would I live?"

Mao Zedong's Tibet policy was aimed at enforcing Chinese hegemony. In 1950, with Communist troops advancing toward Tibet, the delegation of the Dalai Lama had no choice but to sign the "Seventeen-point Agreement." Its essential effect was twofold: first, to enlist the Tibetan army into the People's Liberation Army so as to ensure that the Chinese could enter Tibet "peacefully"; second, to take over Tibet's power. Indeed, the Seventeen-point Agreement is redolent of the colonial unequal treaties [which China was once forced to sign]. Through this agreement, Mao assumed all power over Tibet and ultimately forced socialist reform. Actually the Chinese government itself did not comply with and carry out the agreement. Not only was Tibetan's social system altered and their religious life disturbed, but they interfered in all aspects of the Tibetan lives. The Tibetans' indignation and hatred toward the Chinese government finally led to the

1959 rebellion, in which more than eighty-seven thousand Tibetans were killed. According to the Tenth Panchen Lama, 10 to 15 percent of the Tibetans were eventually arrested. The Dalai Lama himself escaped to India with a hundred thousand followers.

For the past several decades, despite the Chinese government's oppression of Tibet, the Dalai Lama has insisted on the principle of nonviolence. This has gained him worldwide support. His winning the Nobel Peace Prize in 1989 not only greatly encouraged the Tibetan people's efforts toward freedom and independence but also inspired the Chinese who were fighting for democracy.

Faced with such international support for the Tibetans, in 1992 the Chinese government felt obliged to issue a *White Paper* on Tibet: "Tibet: Its Ownership and Human Rights." A quarter of the *White Paper* tried to use "historical facts" to prove that Tibet has belonged to China since ancient times, and therefore it is perfectly legitimate for the Chinese to retain sovereignty there. The remainder of the *White Paper* tried to support the slogan "no Communist Party, no new Tibet," boasting about and exaggerating how the Communist Party had changed Tibet from "hell" to "heaven." Today every Chinese who escaped the Chinese dictatorship knows that "no Communist Party, no new Tibet" is a lie. It is simple logic that when all of China was in a terrible predicament, how could conditions in Tibet have been so good?

Unfortunately many Chinese are influenced by the government's propaganda and intoxicated by the idea of a "Great China." It is almost natural for them to follow the government's lead whenever the Tibetan issue is brought up. Chinese nationalism and discrimination against Tibetans formed a strong foundation on which the Chinese could oppose the Tibetan people's pursuit of freedom and self-determination.

Parochial nationalism and blind patriotism feed dictatorship and colonialism. Human history demonstrates that all rulers of dictatorships, such as Hitler, Stalin, Mao Zedong, and Deng Xiaoping, have all acted under the guise of patriotism.

After World War II many people under colonial rule declared

independence. The independence movement become a worldwide trend. One of the recent examples is the Soviet Union. With the collapse of the USSR, Stalin's obligatory "Big Socialist Family" has broken into no less than fifteen countries. Another example is Czechoslovakia. Although the Slovak Republic's economic level was lower than that of the Czechs, the majority of Slovakians still voted for independence, and the Czechs allowed them to be independent. There was no need to resort to military force.

Since 95 percent of the population in the "Tibetan Autonomous Region" is Tibetan, Tibetan people have the right to determine whether to be united with China or to be independent. The Tibetans' efforts for self-determination are part of a worldwide trend. The Chinese government's oppression of Tibetans can only arouse stronger resistance and add fuel to the flames of the independent movement. If we Chinese are truly seeking democracy in China, then we have no reason to oppose self-determination and freedom for the Tibetans. We ourselves were once victims of imperialism, and today we suffer under the Chinese dictatorship; how can we oppose the Tibetans who are trying to shake off the yoke of both communism and colonialism?

# A Letter to Deng Xiaoping

## Wei Jingsheng

*The following was written in 1992 while the author was in prison.*

Mr. Deng Xiaoping:

The propaganda campaign you have launched shows that you are not only dissatisfied with your hand-picked successor but also concerned about the affairs of Tibet, which is under your personal care. Therefore your people have hastily worked out a *White Paper* called *Tibet: Its Ownership and Human Rights Situation* to cover up their incompetence and ignorance—which are also *your* incompetence and ignorance. In order to maintain their position and power, they continue to use old lies and distortions to deceive you and the Chinese people. The result will be that by the time the majority wake up from their dreams, Tibet will no longer be part of China. The domino effect will go far beyond the 1.2 million square kilometers of Tibet; you will become a laughingstock and be condemned by history.

In order to improve the situation and solve the Tibet question, the first thing to do is understand what the problems are. Only listening to soothing lies will not help you understand reality; you will not be able to grasp, much less solve, the problem. I myself know only a little about Tibetan history. I believe, however, that I am more clear-minded than you and your people. Thus I venture to write this letter to you and hope that you will create an academic atmosphere of free expression so that people of knowledge can determine what the problems are and bring more insight to this issue. Only thus can we avoid losing the last opportunity to settle the issue. Otherwise we will be repeating the mistakes of the Soviet Union and Yugoslavia and will suffer the same fate.

The Tibet issue is a difficult one because of the area's uniqueness and the vagueness of its sovereignty. In fact, established international law is no longer applicable, and many parts of it are mutually contradictory and cannot be relied on to judge the more complicated matters of today's world order. Over-reliance of this outdated and nonbinding international law will not in any way help solve the problem we face today. For instance, in reality, Canada and Australia enjoy total independence and sovereignty. It would be ludicrous for us to define them as British colonies, much less British territories, by arguing that the head of state of these two countries is the queen of the United Kingdom and top government officials must be approved by the queen. In order to solve problems, people should face reality and not try to find "evidence and facts" only from history books.

The issue of Tibet is unique and more complicated than the above-mentioned cases. The "unity" between Tibet and China (Qing dynasty and Republic of China) is so special that many scholars do not comprehend it. The authors of the White Paper are worse than other scholars; their arguments have failed to clarify the facts. [For example, contrary to what the White Paper says,] the Golden Urn Lottery System was a method only used by outside forces to settle the power struggle between religious factions. It had nothing to do with administrative control. Were Mr. Liu Bocheng to be invited to help solve your family disputes, Mr. Deng, could it then be said that your family was being controlled by Liu Bocheng and that the Deng family is affiliated with the Liu family? [Applying such reasoning to Tibet] is ignorant and distorts the facts. Your acquaintances Ya Hanzhang and Phuntsog Wanggyal [the latter a Tibetan member of PRC National People's Congress and the father of Wei's former girlfriend] are well aware of all this. But you would not listen to them. Had you done so, you would not have been led astray by the swindlers [around you].

Likewise, the Amban [Chinese representative] in Tibet was posted there as a "liaison officer" after the suppression of the rebellion in Nepal (which was then affiliated with Tibet) to help put down any such rebellions in the future. He was not, as the White Paper claims, the top administrative officer in Tibet appointed after the suppression of the Dzungar Mongol rebellion. His position was not even as high as the governor in a colony. It was something like the British ambassador to Brunei. He consulted and participated in Tibet's military and foreign affairs. He actually never had any authority over Tibet's administrative and military affairs, and his power was far less than that of the British ambassador to Brunei. As admitted by the authors of the White Paper, the forces of the Qing dynasty and Sichuan Province, led by the Amban, were financed by the Qing court as "foreign forces" (*waiguo jundui*). They were not financed by the Tibetan government. The authors of the White Paper failed to mention that this army was called the Amban's armed escort. Should we ever claim that the sovereignty of the European countries was transferred because of the military presence of the United States?

Tibet chose its head of state, set its administrative bodies, and governed itself in its own way. It had its own army, which was commanded by the Tibetan government. This shows that Tibet was a sovereign country, unlike Croatia or Ukraine, which indeed lost their sovereignty. Even had Tibet lost its sovereignty, it still would have had the right to free itself from the suzerain state. "No one has ever recognized Tibet as an independent country." What role can such an argument play in solving the problem? It may convince some college students, but it is useless in understanding and solving the problem. Whether you admit it or not, the reality is plain to see. So you would be wiser to respect the rights of the other side. At least then you could win some trust.

Tibet had a special status: although it did not lose its sovereignty, it was not an entirely independent country. But even though it was not independent, it was not a colony either. It was not taking care of all its affairs as an independent sovereign country; at the same time it was not ruled as a province of China by an appointee of the Qing court. In truth Tibet had total autonomy over its domestic affairs while being part of the Qing Empire with regard to its foreign affairs. Because of these complex arrangements, many Chinese and foreigners do not know all the facts and thus considered Tibet a province of China. Similar cases of this kind of union were rare. From a legal standpoint, it resembled the Commonwealth or the new European Community. What is common in these situations is that the people identified themselves with the same leadership (the United Kingdom, Europe, and China) while at the same time identifying themselves with their respective independent countries. The unity is voluntary; the countries concerned reserve the right to break away. In the case of a commonwealth, the unity of the kingdoms normally leads to sovereignty. In the case of the European Community, democratic unity on an equal basis has led to a voluntary unity of sovereign countries. Tibet and [Qing] China enjoyed a unity of two sovereignties resulting from mutual agreement between the two supreme authorities. Thus neither the European-type unity of today nor the China–Tibet unity of Qing times has legal [sovereignty] implications.

According to the agreement and to customary practice, the Qing court would send troops to Tibet only at the request of the Dalai Lama and would return to Sichuan and Qinghai immediately after finishing the tasks the Dalai Lama had specified. No permanent Chinese army was in Tibet; only certain forces under the command of the Amban were stationed in designated barracks. The Qing court was partly responsible for Tibet's external and military affairs and was in charge, on an irregular basis, of the security of Tibet and the repression of rebellions. For their part, the Dalai Lama's religious institutions were entrusted with the major task of maintaining the unity of the Qing Empire. The Dalai Lama played the role of the supreme spiritual leader of the state religion of the Qing Empire. He was not like the "imperial teacher" in ancient times; he was the supreme spiritual leader of the national religion and enjoyed a popularity surpassing even that of the emperor in three quarters of the Qing territory (Tibet, Xinjiang, Qinghai, Gansu, Sichuan, Yunnan, part of Burma, Inner and Outer Mongolia, and provinces in the Northeast and part of the Russian Far East). In fact the first emperor of the Qing dynasty made lamaism the state religion precisely because "in order to rule the various areas of Mongolia, it is necessary to embrace Lamaism." Lamaism became the main force maintaining the unity of the empire when it had the largest territory in history. The Qing court, in turn, with its military force and huge financial support, helped the Dalai Lama maintain his supreme position and power, as well as territorial sovereignty over much more territory than the present Tibet [Autonomous Region].

In this union, each side became the main precondition for the continuing existence of the other; the word *tremendous* could hardly describe the benefit each side obtained from this unity. The union was stable and durable. The legal status of the two sides was equal, although the real power of the two sides diverged. Appointing a minister to Tibet and sending large quantities of supplies there were ways to maintain the equilibrium of relations between the two sides. Otherwise the influence of the religious leader would have surpassed that of the emperor, at the expense of the equilibrium and equality of the two sides. True, relations between the Qing court and Tibet underwent many changes over the years, but this basic pattern was maintained until late in the Qing dynasty and relations between the two sides remained stable throughout the period. For this reason, Tibet did not break away from China in the way that Korea, Vietnam, Laos, Burma, and Mongolia eventually did. Tibet stood firmly on the Chinese side even when British troops occupied Lhasa.

This was primarily because the voluntary unity was based on common interest in accordance with the laws of humanity, which reflects the principle that "the people's interest is the supreme interest." Nothing other than this principle can explain the stability of the relationship. Compare this to what has happened in the Soviet Union and Yugoslavia. Elsewhere, people who even speak the same language have formed different countries. Do we disagree over the fact that the United States, the United Kingdom, Ireland, Australia, and Canada are separate sovereign countries? The will and aspirations of the people are the main constituting factor of sovereignty. An element of sovereignty would be lost with the loss of the aspiration for self-rule of a certain portion of the people. Other conditions, as defined by the so-called law of sovereignty, must be based on people's aspirations for self-rule and national self-determination. Without this essential basis, other forms of "sovereignty" will eventually lose their validity. Military occupation and administrative control cannot change this principle, especially in our time.

So relations between Tibet and China were established on the basis of a unity that did not rely on military occupation and administrative rule but on the aspiration for self-rule and national self-determination. Thus the relationship was stable for a long time. From the mid-nineteenth to the mid-twentieth century, China failed to fulfill its commitment to security in Tibet because of the weakness of China itself. Still, the government of the Dalai Lama respected the treaties between the two sides and did nothing to jeopardize unity. Given China's internal turmoil and foreign powers encouraging Tibet to declare independence, Tibet, had it attempted to "split," could have easily done so—as did Mongolia.

The *White Paper* states that no country ever recognized Tibet as independent. This is not true. During the period when Britain ruled India, especially at the time of the Simla Convention (1914), a seat was reserved for Tibet as an independent country. Thus the attempt to establish the independence of Tibet was not successful only because the Dalai Lama's government declined. The protest lodged by the representative of the weak Chinese government did not carry as much weight as has been claimed. At the time, when the Chinese government had long failed to fulfill its obligations, and large areas of Tibet were occupied by or affiliated with foreign countries, the position of the Dalai Lama government was even more estimable.

For a number of reasons relations between China and Tibet became estranged during this period. First, China was becoming a modern society and the influence of religion was declining. Religion was no longer so important as it had been during the Yuan, Ming, and early Qing dynasties, though we should still not underestimate its influence. Second, China had become so weak that it could hardly afford to take care of its western neighbor, and Tibet had already learned to defend itself. The military assistance from China was no longer a necessity and, at any rate, could no longer be relied on. Third, the previously close trade relations between Tibet and China were gradually being undermined by commodities coming into Tibet from Britain and India. Fourth, Chinese culture lost its appeal to the neighboring countries and regions, so the cultural link between China and such places as Tibet became greatly weakened. In the process of this drifting apart, the separation between the *peoples* was even greater than that between the *governments*; nothing could be more profound than the estrangement of the mind. To the Tibetans, deceit (mostly of the people of Sichuan Province and of the Muslims [Hui] in northwest China) had replaced the image of Chinese as allies and defenders. In the minds of the Chinese, who considered themselves an enlightened people, the perceived backwardness and ignorance of the "half human, half beast" Tibetans had replaced their image as subjects of the living Buddha. Although this mutual prejudice did not cause an immediate constitutional split, it laid the foundation for the retaliatory killings by both sides in subsequent days and portended a possible split in the future. And who is the director of this tragedy? None other than you, Mr. Deng.

As early as the 1940s Tibet's ruling class started to discuss social reform there. They wanted a social system like that in Britain or India, a moderate reform based on religious values. Consistent with the custom over several thousand years, they wanted to carry out the reform by themselves. They did not like the idea of being reformed by foreigners or quasi-foreign Han [ethnic Chinese]. The Chinese Nationalists managed to respect this tradition so that relations between the Guomindang and Tibet were relatively harmonious. Furthermore, the Tibetan people did not want revolution—fighting landlords and killing class enemies to redistribute land. This [moderate approach] reflected not only the will of the ruling class but the will of the entire society. The chanting that "liberated serfs look forward to the coming of the Communist Party" is but a slogan in your propaganda. In no way does it describe the true feelings of any serfs at that time. You might as well ask your old subordinates Ya Hanzhang and Phuntsog Wanggyal about the "great achievements" of the Communists in inciting Tibetan serfs. You will understand then that I am being objective. In fact, in most countries the toughest obstacle to the [revolutionary] liberation of serfs came from the serfs themselves. This was the case in Germany and Russia. It was because of the common will of Tibetans and the practices of the [Tibetan] Communists that the Tibetan government did not oppose cooperation with the Chinese Nationalists, but firmly refused to let the Chinese Communists enter Tibet. They even expelled the Tibetan Communist Party led by Phuntsog Wanggyal, because they believed that he represented the Chinese. All this proves that Tibet at that time exercised total sovereignty (even in foreign affairs and national defense). The subsequent arrangement of the return of the Sichuan army and the Tibetan Communist Party from India was made through diplomatic channels.

During that period [the late 1940s] the Chinese Communist Party was at its height. Like all other communist parties, it had little respect for sovereignty and national self-determination. Meanwhile, India, which had just gained independence from British rule, could hardly afford to help Tibet in its struggle against the Chinese Communists. Therefore the Tibetans' attempt to deny the Communists entry into Tibet ended in failure. Moreover, the inexperience of the young Dalai Lama and the corruption of the Tibetan bureaucracy were the major factors in the Communist troops' smooth occupation of Lhasa. Mr. Deng, your decision—and that of Mao Zedong—to carry out the "peaceful liberation" of Tibet should be deemed a correct policy, although it does resemble an agreement reached under the pressure of a heavy military presence, which, according to international law, should be rendered invalid. If this policy had been *implemented* properly, the government of the Dalai Lama might have accepted it, the sovereign unity of China and Tibet might have continued, and the international community would have had to accept it as a fait accompli. Thus Tibet would not have become such a headache for China. Tibetans are a trustworthy people and are not adept at playing tricks.

Regretfully, the leaders of the Chinese Communist Party, Mao Zedong, and you yourself became big-headed with the "victory" of the Korean War and the improved economy. Later, when you carried out the Great Leap Forward and the ultra-leftist policies in China proper, you began to implement leftist policies in Tibet—accelerating the "democratic reform" there. By so doing, you effectively tore up the "Agreement on the Peaceful Liberation of Tibet." This caused anger among Tibetans of all walks of life. A people's war (the 1959 Tibetan uprising) broke out against the leftist policies of the Communist Party, under the banner of fighting against outsiders and foreign religion. The Chinese government considered this a rebellion. During the war and for a long period afterward, the mutual discrimination and prejudice between the Tibetans and Chinese added to the hatred that caused so many innocent people to be killed by the army, as well as suffer torture by officials. The estrangement between the two peoples deepened, and the Tibetan national struggle for independence escalated. To talk about sovereignty under these circumstances would only make people believe that the Communist Party planned to continue these practices. The situation and the pattern of confrontation between the two sides was just like that between the colonial powers and the colonies in the old days. It is also like the situation in today's Yugoslavia.

Let us now examine two recent examples in the world—one positive, the other negative. The first is Yugoslavia. Like you, Yugoslavia's leaders would not recognize other peoples' right to national self-determination and even resorted to armed force to prevent other peoples from gaining such rights. But it could never achieve its goal; instead it instilled tremendous hatred with its attendant long-term costs. The other example is Russia, which respected the right to self-determination and autonomy of other nationalities but managed to maintain the Commonwealth of Independent States (CIS). There has remained room for possible future unity, for the traditional trust and good feelings have lasted. The difference between the two situations will become more evident as time passes. Serbia was in a far better position than Russia. In the past, Russia had caused far more grievances among other nationalities than Serbia had. However, differences in handling the questions have resulted in different consequences. The major dissimilarity is that Russia abided by the law governing human society and respected the right of other nations to self-determination and autonomy. Factors in favor of unity have therefore been able to play a role.

Although in modern human society the trend toward unity is stronger than that toward division, overemphasis of the sovereignty and administrative authority of one nationality over others is actually detrimental to unity. The societies that have already split or are in the process of division are those that insisted on unlimited administrative power of one nation over other nations. The toughest obstacle facing societies that have already achieved unity or are in the process of achieving it is likewise resisting the temptation to overemphasize sovereignty. The advantage of unity is obvious, but the arguments against it are also strong. Why should people emphasize only the arguments against unity? Can you find a case to show that unity was successfully maintained by extreme pressure? Even if you could offer an example, it would be because the time for division has not yet come. All along you have advocated anticolonialism and national independence. In fact, you do not understand what anticolonialism and national independence are. You use them only as convenient tools; you do not genuinely believe in them. This is precisely the root cause of your leftism.

The relationship between China and Tibet is much better than what existed between the Soviet Union and Yugoslavia. Until 1949 China had never oppressed Tibet nor had it forced Tibet to become a subject of China. The two sides had achieved sovereign[1] unity voluntarily. Even today, the chances of unity between

China and Tibet are much better than that within the CIS and the European Community. In the early days of his forced exile, the Dalai Lama did not demand independence, nor is he demanding it today. This shows that a very good chance of unity exists. However, you have adhered to the old ideas and policies and continued the old bureaucratic ways. What you are doing is pushing Tibet toward secession. China has already lost nearly half of our High Qing ancestral territory. Should this go on, our later generations will have to make a living by exporting labor, and revitalizing the Chinese nation would be out of the question.

Thus it is still possible to overcome the evil consequences caused by the suppression and killings of the last forty years. To return the China–Tibet relationship to the traditional track of normal development, the most pressing tasks are the following:

First, mutual hatred and prejudice between the Han people and the Tibetans must be rooted out, especially the Hans' erroneous notions about the Tibetans. As a result of the propaganda of the past forty years, cadres in Tibet (and in other areas, too) have a deep-rooted prejudice against the Tibetans, which in turn has deepened the Tibetans' hatred of the Hans. The real situation in this regard is beyond your imagination, and it is not at all like what your people have told you. Let me give you a few examples to help you understand the seriousness of the problem.

My parents did not know any Tibetans and never conducted any research about Tibet. Whatever they knew about Tibet was what the Communist Party had told them. In their minds Tibetans were half-human, half-beast. So it was only natural that when I planned to marry a Tibetan girl, they expressed the strongest opposition and even threatened to sever all relations with me. Later on, when they got to know the girl, they changed their views. However, the girl's parents would not tolerate in-laws like my parents, and I did not become the son-in-law of this Tibetan family.

My second example is this: When I was imprisoned in Tibet (Qinghai) I overheard many conversations that helped me to appreciate the Han cadres' prejudice against Tibetans. Anything that had something to do with Tibet was looked down on. For instance, Tibetan dogs are renowned. But Han cadres preferred to raise dogs they bought in China proper. They would laugh at me when I told them how good Tibetan dogs were. They were convinced of what I said only when it was shown on TV that foreigners would pay a lot of money for a Tibetan dog. Further, they would not believe that Tibetan butter was the same as butter in a Western restaurant. How could it be possible that old Tibetans eat the same thing as foreigners? And Yak meat is most delicious, but the Han cadres in Tibet would say, "As there is nothing else to eat, we have to buy yak meat." When a Tibetan doctor learned that I enjoyed yak meat and wanted to buy some Tibetan butter for me, he was surprised at first but then took me for one of his own people. These illustrations show how the Communist cadres have thought about and treated the Tibetans. It is even worse than white people's discrimination against Native Americans. Frankly, you yourselves have engendered this prejudice against the Tibetans; it is reflected in all the relevant documents, statements, and other propaganda materials. This has deepened the estrangement between the Han people and the Tibetans and is very decisive.

Overcoming the grievances accumulated over forty years is going to be extremely difficult. However, efforts should be made every day to this end. All nationalities should be treated equally. There should be no special preferences because these indicate that someone is treated like an outsider. Cadres at various levels who do not respect national minorities should be replaced. Han chauvinism should be eliminated from all publications. Over the past forty years people have tended to mistake narrow nationalism and national chauvinism for patriotism. Whenever Princess Wen Cheng is mentioned, people regard her as China's savior of Tibet. This is too much; it is not in accordance with history. The labor camp in Qinghai to which I was sent was in the place where the Tibetan army defeated the 100,000 troops led by General Xue Rengui. As a result, Princess Wen Cheng was married to the Tibetan king as a peace offering. [This is an error; the two were married before the battle.—Eds.] None of the cadres in that region knew the story, however. They all believed that the Tibetans were "enlightened" because of the Chinese princess. They even thought that they themselves were in Tibet to help the Tibetans reclaim barren land—yet this is where the Tibetans had lived for generations. They acted and talked just like colonizers. It is your one-sided propaganda that has resulted in this national prejudice against the Tibetans. This mentality should be changed, together with the elimination of the practice of the authors of the *White Paper*, who are used to talking big and telling lies.

The second task needing prompt attention is for the government to speed up the development of the market economy in Tibet and establish closer economic relations between China proper and the Tibetan market. A century ago British and Indian commodities had much success in penetrating the Tibetan market. Yet in the past forty-odd years, the Tibetan market has suffered great damage. The so-called socialist planned price that was fixed for the products of Tibet's mineral resources and livestock, something that resembles colonialist exploitation, has caused tremendous loss to the Tibetan economy. Your "aid" could in no way make up for their loss. What is more, most of your "aid" has been used to support the apparatus of suppression or scientific research of the Hans. These include government offices of various levels, hospitals, and hotels for the Hans, military facilities, observatories, and geothermal power plants—certainly not what the Tibetan economy needs most.

No matter what excuses you give the Tibetan people, they are not as stupid as you think. They know you are not sincere in your offers to help them, so they will not trust you. The decision makers should treat Tibet as if it were their own homeland and make good use of financial assistance to help Tibet's economic development most efficiently. The various barriers and "managed prices" should be eliminated, and Tibetan commodities should have easier access to the markets in China proper; indeed they should be given preferential prices. Efforts should also be made to improve economic and trade relations between Tibet and other areas of the PRC. This is most important in consolidating the Tibet–Han relationship.

Third, the Chinese government should do away the traditional policy of detaining Tibetan religious leaders as hostages. Both religious and nonreligious Tibetans have a strong aversion to this policy, a policy that can hardly prove your respect for human rights. The Chinese government should stop thinking in terms of the so-called great Han empire and sit at the negotiating table with the Dalai Lama. He is concerned about your sincerity; in the past you never won his trust. You should therefore let him choose the place for the negotiation. He should be allowed to return to Lhasa if he so chooses. All these are reasonable, basic conditions. Your position has been incomprehensible; there is no reason why you should not agree to all this. Even today, the appointment of the Dalai Lama's negotiating aides has to be approved by the Chinese government. Isn't that just too much? To come up with all sorts of excuses to postpone negotiations is an indication that your people have no confidence in themselves. They seem afraid that if sincere negotiations really got under way, all their nonsense would be exposed in the glare of the light.

By continuing to tolerate their defiance of law and public opinion, you are rewarding your cronies at the expense of the national interest. If you agree to negotiations, you will greatly improve the chances of Tibet remaining part of China. Negotiations should start with no preconditions. It would be wise to invite the Dalai Lama to return to Lhasa. It would be better than having him surrounded by extremists. In fact the Dalai Lama knows that without an alliance with China, he would face the ambitious Indians who are no better than the Chinese. Sikkim [annexed by India in 1975], Bhutan, and Nepal [both pressured by India] are good examples for a future independent Tibet. If we could do a better job, why should the Tibetans invite suffering for themselves by breaking away from the unity that has existed for several centuries?

The trend of the modern world is unity; it will happen sooner or later. The advantages of unity overshadow its disadvantages. From the Dalai Lama's actions in recent years, I believe he understands the realities better than I do. But he has his own problems; we should not press him too hard.

## Note

1. At this point Wei actually used the term *zhuquan lianhe*. *Lianhe* means "unity." Wei is apparently referring to his theory of dual sovereignty (*zhuquan*) mentioned above, but in this essay his use of the terms *sovereign* and *sovereignty* is not always clear, in part because *sovereignty* and *sovereignties* are written the same way in Chinese.—Eds.

# My View on the Tibet Issue

## Harry Wu

When Deng Xiaoping came to power in the late 1970s he put forward his now well-known policies calling for the modernization of China's industry, agriculture, national defense, and science and technology. These became known as the Four Modernizations. Then, in the winter of 1979, a young Beijing electrician named Wei Jingsheng expressed dissatisfaction with the idea and advanced the notion that China needed a *fifth* modernization, namely, political modernization, the main component of which was democracy. For this "crime" he was locked up for several years in Beijing, and then transferred to the Thirteenth Laogai Farm, a forced labor camp in Amdo, where the majority of the residents are Tibetans. We Chinese know the area as Qinghai Province. Wei was confined there for four and a half years. Later, on the basis of this experience, he wrote his well-known letter to Deng Xiaoping regarding the patriarch's policy on Tibet. [The letter is reproduced in this volume as Selection 5.—Eds.]

In 1991 I went to China from the United States to investigate and expose the darkness of China's gulag. During that investigation I made a special point of visiting the Thirteenth Laogai Farm. I went there not only because Wei Jingsheng had once been jailed there but also because the camp was located in the Qaidam Basin. This part of Qinghai, along with the Tarim Basin of Xinjiang, is called "China's Siberia." Like the outlying, desolate Siberia of Russia, the two northwestern regions became natural prisons where about one million convicts have been jailed by the Beijing authorities since the 1950s. Many among them are "felony" political prisoners.

From Xining, the capital of Qinghai Province, I went to the west toward the Thirteenth Laogai Camp, crossing over the mountain [known to Tibetans as Ninda La and to us Chinese as] Riyue. When I reached the crest of Mt. Riyue, beside a tent for travelers to rest I found a stone tablet on which was engraved a bit of history. China's Princess Wen Cheng's marriage to the Tibetan king, Songsten Gampo, had taken place in the year 641, and Princess Wen Cheng had crossed these mountains on her way to Tibet. "Upon arriving here, Princess Wen Cheng performed a farewell ceremony that included a bath, a fast, and a kowtow to the East—in farewell to her country and family. After the ceremony, the princess changed to Tibetan dress and went to Tibet escorted by a squad of guards of the Tibetan king." History, as recorded on the tablet, shows that the marriage of Princess Wen Cheng and the Tibetan king Songsten Gampo was not the marriage of an emperor's daughter to a general of the emperor's subordinate province; rather, it was a political marriage between two equal countries. As I read this tablet, I realized I was standing on the old border which had demarcated two sovereign nations, Tibet and China.

This was quite different from what I had learned about the history of Tibet and Sino–Tibetan relations since my childhood. Both the Chinese Republican government before 1949 and the Chinese Communist government after 1949 had told me that our country was composed of five nationalities: Han, Manchu, Mongolian, Hui (Chinese Muslim), and Tibetan; we had a vast territory of 9.6 million square kilometers and a rich civilization of five thousand years. This empire, which included what is now the People's Republic of Mongolia, was engraved on my mind in the shape of a mulberry leaf.

I considered myself a patriotic young man. I used to recite patriotic poems by the poet Lu You. When I had occasion to visit the city of Hangzhou, I would take pictures of the tablet on which was engraved the famous patriotic General Yue Fei's phrase of loyalty to our country. So when China recognized the independence of "Outer Mongolia" in 1950, I might as well have been hit by a cudgel. It was difficult for me to accept the separation; I saw it as a piece cut off from the beautiful mulberry leaf. Then only a teenager, I believed that the separation of Mongolia from China was a national shame and a plot by the Soviet imperialists.

In the 1950s, when I attended college in Beijing, I learned that Mongolia had been altogether independent since 1924, though China had not accepted the fact. It was only after Mao established Communist China that, under the pressure of the Soviet Union, China reluctantly recognized the People's Republic of Mongolia. In fact, to this day, the Republic of China on Taiwan has never recognized "Outer Mongolia" as an independent country, even though the People's Republic of Mongolia has long been a member of the United Nations and is recognized by almost all nations around the world. Maps of China printed in Taiwan still show my great mulberry leaf.

Before coming to the United States in 1985, I had never doubted that Tibet was part of China, and I had never heard of the Tibetans' separatist movement. When I learned, soon after my arrival, that Tibetans were seeking independence, my first response was that it might be another imperialist plot, with someone else wanting to cut off another piece of the mulberry leaf. When I heard more about the independence movement, I began to wonder if Tibet really is part of China, so I began to read books on the subject. I learned that the real history of Tibet is quite different from what I was taught by the two Chinese governments.

Even *The Atlas of Chinese History Maps*, published by the Chinese Social Science Institute in Beijing, clearly shows that Tibet was an independent country and never a part of China at least before 1280, when the Mongols established what we Chinese call the Yuan dynasty. The Beijing government and most of the Chinese people use the Yuan dynasty's rule over Tibet as historical "proof" of China's sovereignty over Tibet. It is obvious that the Yuan dynasty was a Mongol empire that included most Asian countries such as China, Korea, Vietnam, as well as Tibet.

After the demise of the Yuan dynasty, the Ming dynasty reestablished the Chinese Empire. However, its authority was largely limited to China proper; it had little or no control over the Northwest, the Northeast, or Tibet. The lands to the north and northeast of China were inhabited by the Manchu people, who had an alliance with the Mongols, and the Tibetans also joined in this political and religious alliance. When the alliance, dominated by the Manchus, overthrew the Ming dynasty and established the Qing, that dynasty became suzerain over Mongolia and Tibet.

The Revolution of 1911 toppled the Manchu rulers and established the Republic of China. Ironically, while recognizing the abolition of the Qing dynasty, all of China's rulers after the 1911 Revolution, including the founding father of the Republic, Sun Yat-sen, presidents of the Republic of China Chiang Kai-shek, Chiang Ching-kuo, and Lee Teng-hui, and leaders of the People's Republic of China Mao Zedong and Deng Xiaoping, had no doubt that they had inherited the territory of the Qing dynasty and that Tibet was a part of China, as it had been during the Qing dynasty. They have also used slogans, such as "republicanism" for the five nationalities and "autonomy" for minority ethnic groups, to justify the retention of the Qing empire's domain.

In reality, during the Republican period, China had endured separatist warlord regimes, as well as the Japanese invasion and the civil war. The central government was too weak to handle such a vast territory. Therefore, during the period from 1911 to 1950, Tibet was in fact an independent country. But many Chinese historians have accepted the current rulers' stand and have even helped the authorities to instill in the populace a twisted version of history, imbued with Han chauvinism.

However intoxicated the Chinese may be with the idea of a vast Great China, unbiased history books provide us with a different story, at least concerning Tibet; that is, until the Communists took over Tibet, the country had had its own political system, religion, currency, taxation, law, army, and government. Because of its special geographic position and culture, Tibet had little association with the outside world except for some contact with its neighboring countries. The Qing court rarely, if at all, interfered in Tibet's politics, economy, judiciary, and army. Indeed, its respect for Tibet's religion and its material support had greatly helped to stabilize the Tibetan government and to promote a friendly relationship between China and Tibet.

Unfortunately, in 1950 Tibet was occupied by the Chinese Communist army. Communists regard the "liberation of all human beings" as their duty; of course Tibet was part of this responsibility, especially in view of Tibet's "backward culture." Nowhere have Communists allowed religion to flourish. This was to be especially true in Tibet, for Lamaist Buddhism was deemed to be evil.

In his poetry Mao Zedong likened himself to the Tang and Qing emperors (who "unified" China), and his aim was to establish a huge, homogeneous Chinese Empire. Now, since the Communists claimed to have "liberated" Tibetans, they have had to devise a rationale for this "liberation." So the Beijing authorities retroactively condemned Tibet as a barbaric, slave society that had been in need of liberation. True, some aspects of the old Tibetan system were unreasonable, such as the integration of politics and religion and violations of human rights. But has anyone the right to destroy a society by force? Moreover, what has socialism actually done for the Tibetans? Consider the following:

- In Tibet's entire history, never have so many people fled into exile as under the Communists.
- In all of Tibetan history, never has there been such severe destruction of their religion as there is today—six thousand temples were destroyed and hundreds of thousands of monks and nuns were forced to resume secular lives.
- On Tibetan land, never have there been so many Chinese in control of all political power and the country's economic lifeblood;
- Never have there been on Tibetan soil so many prisons and of such enormous size and forced labor camps—as many as twelve according to one investigation.

- Never have there been so many soldiers and police in Tibet as there are today.

While we Chinese are fighting for democracy, freedom, and human rights in our homeland, we must be aware that Tibetan people have the same right to fight for their freedom, democracy, and human rights. Even if Tibet had never been an independent country, the Tibetans would still have the right to choose their own political system, religion, and lifestyle. The descendants of the French in Quebec are not being denounced as "splittists" simply because they seek independence from Canada. I do not believe that a great number of Chinese people would like to live on the Tibet Plateau. Most of them who have gone to Tibet were coerced or deceived. I think any Chinese currently in Tibet should go home, and they should not be used by the government as tools of nationalism.

The Chinese Communist dictatorship is like a plate composed of Beijing, Shanghai, Tibet, Ningxia, Sichuan, and the other provinces and regions. Here live Hans, Manchus, Mongols, Huis, and Tibetans. The breakup of any part of the plate could lead the entire plate to crash. Actually, in terms of the economy, culture, and population of the People's Republic, Tibet does not comprise much of the Communist plate. Nonetheless the Tibetans' fight for freedom and democracy could be a catalyst effecting the disintegration of the entire Communist dictatorship. Isn't that just what our Chinese brothers and sisters need—to smash the shackles of communism?

# Independence and Unification

## Xiang Xiaoji

During the 1980s the Chinese people's awareness of democracy improved greatly, reaching a climax in 1989 with a widespread call for the end of one-party dictatorship. At the same time, Tibet's independence movement, Taiwan's separatist movement, and Hong Kong's autonomous movement all received the attention of the international community. When faced with these new situations, there was no unanimity among Chinese democracy activists, who have often seemed confused or uncertain about their position. National unification may be the only issue on which it is difficult for Chinese democracy activists to speak or act contrary to the Chinese government.

No doubt there would be suspicion of treason were this issue in fact discussed. Under the twin influences of traditional Chinese culture and the culture of the Communist dictatorship, the principles of democracy, freedom, and equality are supposed to be sacrificed in favor of nationalism. This is true not only of democracy activists but also of ordinary people. Some clamor that they are not seeking democracy only to see the country disintegrate. But we must admit that today's so-called unity is indeed the result of the power of dictatorship. The purpose of democracy is not to seek the disintegration of a nation; rather, it is to provide greater room for free choice in people's lives. If the day arrives when people want the nation to break apart, then this would only indicate that the previous unification was a false and painful bondage.

The first event, relating literally to *divorce* in Chinese history, occurred after the Chinese Communists took power and issued the first divorce law. Those who oppose divorce have believed that this law brought on high divorce rates. Clearly this kind of thinking cannot withstand close scrutiny. The purpose of the divorce law was not to encourage divorce and tear families apart but to allow people (especially women) new possibilities that had not existed before but for which many had longed. Some may not agree with this comparison because they think a nation's disintegration is far more complicated and serious than a family breakup, but I do not accept this view. Further, I believe that individual happiness is far more important than a country's unification.

Mainland China's democracy movement, Tibet's independence movement, Taiwan's separatist movement, and Hong Kong's autonomous movement all have something in common: They all seek the end of China's dictatorship. Moreover, among the Tibetan, Taiwanese, and Hong Kong movements, there is also a geographical and historical meeting ground. All three countries are located on China's periphery, and all have a history of not being under the control of the Chinese government. Tibet's independence movement also has its own unique causes—its ethnicity and its religion.

We can perceive from this that the reasons underlying Tibet's independence movement outweigh those of the other movements; in addition, and following from that fact, Tibet has received the most sympathy and support from the international community. Under the domination of the Chinese government, the Tibetans have been under the twin oppressions of human rights and sovereignty deprivation. It is unfortunate that, in the face of practical political interests, no nation has been willing to offend the Chinese government and recognize the Tibetan government-in-exile. Only nongovernmental organizations give the Dalai Lama such high honors. From the perspective of international law, the longer the situation persists, the more difficult Tibet's position becomes. It is predictable from the recent issue of discovering the reincarnation of the Panchen Lama that, after the death of the Dalai Lama, his reincarnation will cause even greater antagonism between the Chinese government and the Tibetans.

In dealing with the issue of unification, the Chinese government usually appeals to nationalism—especially when the audience is foreign. When speaking to its own people, it speaks of stability and uses prosperity and strength as an excuse. Questions such as whether this unification is just, and what the cost of this "prosperity" is, are taboo. In fact "unity" has only one real purpose—to preserve the one-party dictatorship and the interests of the political oligarchy.

The Chinese people's (including the intellectuals') understanding of the Tibet issue is based on the propaganda they have been fed for so long. For example, they have been told that Tibet's slavery system was extremely cruel and that the Chinese government actually "liberated" the Tibetans from all that cruelty. Apparently the Chinese government is not afraid to discuss human rights issues in old Tibet because it believes that Tibet's human rights record was worse than it is now under China's domination. For the moment, we will not discuss whether this is so. The point is that under international law a nation cannot use human rights as the basis for "liberating" a people. When it comes to the Tibet issue, the Chinese government does not raise the point that "human rights is a matter of a people's internal affairs," even though China has insisted on this when its own human rights are questioned by the international community.

The authorities' second line of propaganda is that Tibet's economy was very backward and that the Chinese government has assisted Tibet. Again, whether this is true is a question we will leave aside. If a nation that is highly developed economically can use the notion of assisting another country as the reason for occupying that country, then the Chinese people's resistance to the Japanese occupation in the 1930s was foolish and wrong. At the time, the Japanese raised the idea of a Greater East Asian Co-prosperity Sphere. Why did the Chinese not accept this? If you are going to emphasize your own country's nationalism and national pride, you should also think about other people's national pride. Do not impose on others what you are unwilling to accept yourself.

The third line of propaganda is that for a very long time (at least dating back to the Yuan dynasty) Tibet has been a part of China. In fact, before the Yuan dynasty, Tibet and China were neighboring countries. During the Yuan dynasty, both the Tibetans and Chinese were vassals of the Mongols, who occupied both countries. Strictly speaking, the Yuan dynasty cannot be a part of Chinese history; it is the history of the Mongols. If China can consider the Mongols' colonies as its own, then the United States can consider Canada, Australia, India, and so on, and other former British territories as part of the United States.

The fourth line of propaganda is that if Tibet were drawn out of China's domain, it would fall into the hands of imperialists (probably Britain). This would reduce China's international position. Then Sichuan would find itself no longer a heartland province, but the frontier. The process would continue in this way. This fully exposes China's imperialist thinking; it reminds one of how Stalin and Hitler carved up Poland and relocated Russia's border to the east.

Fifth, the authorities raise the specter of what would happen if Tibet gained its independence and then other ethnic nationalities sought to follow suit. The issue is why would these other ethnic nationalities want independence? In our present world, most countries encompass many nationalities. Not every nationality insists on forming its own nation-state. However, it is under severe oppression that the call for independence of such nationalities arises.

In short, it is unreasonable to use the excuse of the backwardness of politics, economics, and culture to "liberate" and occupy a country. Even Lenin admitted that one cannot use a whip to drive people into heaven. Certainly, the Tibetan people have not been driven to heaven!

The traditional Chinese view is that the more members a family enjoys, the better—and the larger the territory, the better. No matter whether it is country or family, disintegration is always forbidden. Unification is the highest principle. It does not matter whether something has always belonged to me, as long as it comes under my control it cannot ever break away. The hegemony mind-set is strong. If people and organizations of the democracy movement place the principle of unification above the principle of freedom, then this "democracy movement" is deficient. The principles of democracy, freedom, and equality apply not only to a nation's internal affairs but to its foreign relations as well. Indeed, this is a good test for a developing democracy. Only if there is the freedom to separate can genuine unification be possible. This is like setting up a company, signing a contract, and registering for a marriage license. If there is no law on a company's dissolution, dissolving a contract, or dissolving a marriage, then who would dare to set up a company, sign a contract, or find a spouse? Such logic of everyday living also applies to resolving relationships among nationalities and among countries.

In the past five decades the Chinese government's effective occupation of Tibet and the less than full recognition of this occupation by the international community have not impeded the Tibetans' struggle for independence. I hope that the future Chinese democratic government abides by the principles of equality and the spirit of freedom and will consult with the Tibetans on how to resolve the issue of Tibetan independence. We must allow the Tibetans to decide whether they want to remain a part of China or break away from China. The result must reflect the genuine will of the Tibetan people.

# Ripple on the River of History

## Xue Wei

*The following is the text of a speech to the Second International Conference in Support of Tibet, in Bonn, Germany, on June 14, 1996.*

Among the overseas Chinese dissidents and Chinese students, the overwhelming majority regard the Tibetan people's suffering and struggle for human rights with sympathy and support. Although some are skeptical about Tibetan independence or actually opposed to it to varying degrees, this does not obscure our general support for the Tibetans' struggle against tyranny. As activists for democracy, we stand at the forefront of an era. First, we must let people know that the urgent task at hand is to attempt to end the dictatorship of the Chinese Communists, reform China's social system, and then realize democracy, freedom, human rights, and the rule of law. Only under such conditions can the people have the opportunity and requisites to decide what kind of society and political system they want.

In recent years Chinese democracy activists have been concerned about the issue of Tibet. Based on many discussions and observations, some of us have reached the following conclusions: First, based on the principle of democracy, we believe the Tibetan people have the right to decide their own fate and way of life. The right to self-determination is affirmed; other nationalities cannot decide for them. Second, according to the principle of peace, we oppose the use of violence as a solution to the question of separation. The army should absolutely not be used to massacre unarmed people. Third is the principle of transition. If there is currently a great chasm on the question of separation that cannot be solved, then there can be long-term negotiations. At the outset, China must allow Tibet to realize a high level of self-autonomy. During this period of high-level self-government, under the conditions of harmony and mutual respect, the Chinese and Tibetans can discuss further solutions. Over the period of the discussions, as we befriend each other, learn mutual understanding, and enjoy mutual benefits, one may find that separatism is no longer so important. If such conditions exist for a long time and the people of Tibet still want independence and feel that being neighbors is better than being brothers and sisters, they will still have the right to determine their own future by means of a plebiscite. China's future democratic government must respect the Tibetan people's choice.

Overseas Chinese democracy activists are fond of the following saying: "Without a democratic China, there can be no separation. Once China is democratic, there is no need for separation." This slogan naturally has its own rationale and it may or may not be true. Still, only the Tibetans have the right to determine their own fate. Many years in the past, the world was much more divided than now; many years in the future there may well be a world commonwealth, a global village. The unification or separation we pursue today is only a ripple on the river of history. The highest principle that we pursue should be freedom of choice and the true will of the people. I have said that a marriage stems from mutual consent; willingness on the part of both husband and wife is necessary. Yet divorce can occur when only one side insists on breaking up. Further, a marriage without the freedom of divorce can leave people apprehensive.

This past February, I visited Tibet's government-in-exile in Dharamsala, India. I met with the Dalai Lama, members of the government, and Tibetans who fled Tibet both early on and more recently. What amazed me was this little town's rare virtues. The Tibetans have established the world's most virtuous government. The officials all live frugal lives, making sacrifices for their religion and ideas. Many foreign friends have gone there to do voluntary work for the Tibetan refugees, and many Tibetans from Tibet have sent their children to be educated at Dharamsala.

One innocent young Tibetan girl asked me, "When you hear us shout 'China out of Tibet' at protest meetings, do you get mad?" I laughed awkwardly and replied that I am not China, I am a Chinese. Actually I understood her question. The China to which she referred was Communist China, as well as the Communist officials who oppress Tibetans and the army that massacred the people of Tibet. The real people of China and Tibet are friends. In the future we will be good neighbors or even brothers and sisters.

# Federalism and the Future of Tibet

## Yan Jiaqi

The Tibetan problem is a serious, long-term dispute. Early in the 1950s the Chinese Communist Party (CCP) forced through "socialist reform" in the regions of Qinghai province (the approximate equivalent of Amdo) and Chamdo (Kham), causing large numbers of Tibetans from these regions to flee. After the Communist forces arrived in the capital, the people in the Lhasa region daily faced the constant threat of forced "reform." In March 1959 they broke out in a spontaneous protest movement: roughly ten thousand people surrounded the Narbulingka—the Dalai Lama's residence—determined to protect him. Chinese Communist troops dispersed the crowds by force. Confronted with the Tibetan people's unplanned and spontaneous protest, the CCP authorities in Beijing looked for an excuse to suppress it and eventually labeled the protest an "armed rebellion by reactionary Tibetan forces." Afterward the troops stationed in Tibet received instructions to "put down the insurrection." Between March 1959 and March 1962 the struggling Tibetan people were subject to the Communists' suppression: more than sixty thousand fled Tibet for Nepal and India. During the Cultural Revolution the devastation in Tibet forced tens of thousands more Tibetans to leave their homeland; they ended up not only in India and Nepal but also in Europe and North America.

Since the end of the 1970s, and especially after Hu Yaobang's and Wan Li's inspections of Tibet, recognition arose of the seriousness of mistakes in the Party's policies in Tibet, and the policies were revised. At that time Tibet began to put into practice reform and "opening up," along with a series of special policies and flexible measures. Large numbers of Chinese cadres returned to China proper, and a number of Tibetan cadres were able to win promotion. Religious restrictions were lifted and monasteries were restored. But the authorities in Beijing still insisted on labeling the 1959 incident an armed rebellion by Tibetan "reactionary forces," and they used all kinds of measures to prevent the Dalai Lama and the exiled Tibetan people from returning to their homeland.

Focusing on the problem of Tibet's future, serious differences still exist between the party authorities in Beijing and the Dalai Lama's representatives.

## The Dalai Lama's Position on the Future of Tibet

Since 1979 the Tibetan government-in-exile in Dharamsala has had several discussions with Beijing in order to resolve the Tibetan problem. The Tibetans put forward suggestions and initiatives on these and other occasions. In 1982 and 1984 the Dalai Lama sent two delegations to the leadership in Beijing to hold exploratory talks. In Washington in September 1987 the Dalai Lama put forward the Five-point Peace Plan to resolve the Tibetan problem. In June 1988, in Strasbourg, the Dalai Lama produced an even more detailed proposal on the future of Tibet. In London, in December 1991, he published for the first time a statement on the problem of the transition of power in a future Tibet. In an interview with *New York Newsday* in April 1994 he again upheld the principle of nonviolence and published an important statement on relations with China.

These statements from the Dalai Lama include the following points:

- The demilitarization of the entire Tibetan territory, allowing Tibet to be transformed into a peace zone.[1]
- A basic law would be enacted for Tibet. A democratic government would be established, in which politics and religion would be separated. The Tibetan government would be empowered to make decisions on matters relating both to Tibet and to the Tibetan people.[2]
- The production or storage of nuclear weapons and waste in Tibet would be prohibited. Special measures would be taken to protect Tibet's environment, allowing Tibet to become the largest "nature reserve" in the world.[3]
- Tibet would become an autonomous democratic political entity and operate as such in its dealings with the People's Republic of China; "the government of the PRC could continue to be responsible for Tibet's foreign policies, but the Tibetan government should develop and maintain through its own foreign office religious, trade, educational, cultural, tourist, scientific, sporting, and other nonpolitical links. Tibet should participate in international organizations relevant to these matters."[4]
- Regarding the relations between the Chinese and Tibetan peoples within Tibet, such as the problem of the immigration of Chinese to Tibet, we "simply want a stable number of Chinese, who can speak Tibetan and who respect Tibetan culture; the problem of the Chinese and Tibetan people getting along with each other could then be resolved."[5]
- In all matters, the principle of nonviolence would prevail.

Beijing's reaction to the Dalai Lama's suggestions has been to declare that only when the Dalai Lama "stops carrying out activities to split the motherland" and gives up his platform of "Tibetan independence" can negotiations be held. Pursuant to that, on September 2, 1991, the Tibetan government-in-exile announced that "because China's present leadership lacks the will and sincerity to resolve this problem," the proposals put forward to members of the European Parliament in Strasbourg are withdrawn.[6]

## Origins of the Idea of "Tibetan Independence"

The notion of "Tibetan independence" has historical origins. Tibetans and Chinese lived in different regions, and for a long time Tibet had its own armies, managed its own taxation, and laid down its own legal codes. The central government (i.e., China) focused only on its power over foreign relations and did not acknowledge that Tibet had the right to sign treaties with foreign countries of its own accord. During the Qing period (1644–1911), the number of Chinese soldiers stationed in Tibet was very small, and only under circumstances of foreign aggression and civil war would armies be dispatched to Tibet. Relations between Tibet and the central government were not the same as those between the central government and the provinces of China proper. When the Chinese central government planned to impose the pattern of government of Chinese regions on the Tibetan people, the latter were determined to resist. The corruption of the central government and its oppression of the people also gave rise to the idea of independence among the Tibetan people.

At the end of the Qing dynasty, Zhao Erfeng, the governor of Sichuan, undertook a "land redistribution" in the border areas of Xikang between Sichuan and Tibet, with rotating [*liudong*—literally, flowing] government posts replacing the hereditary *tusi* and *tuguan* systems. In practical terms this would have taken the "unified politico-religious" government of the Dalai Lama and transformed it into a regular Chinese province, with the central government exercising jurisdiction over all levels of political power. In his "reforms" Zhao Erfeng had no regard for the Tibetan people's religious faith, and he intruded on their freedom of religion and political authority. When the Tibetans rose up in resistance, he sent large armies into action to suppress them. In 1909, Zhao Erfeng took the post of "minister" (*dachen*) of Tibet. On February 12, 1909, the Sichuan armies reached Lhasa just as the people were taking part in a great religious festival. The Sichuanese troops opened fire, killing both Tibetan monks and lay people, but two years later the troops were expelled. The Communists' "reforms" of the 1950s and 1960s and Zhao Erfeng's "reform" at the end of the Qing dynasty differed in their approach and direction, but the effect of each was similar. Just as the Thirteenth Dalai Lama had once fled to India in 1959, the Fourteenth Dalai Lama followed in his footsteps.

The disintegration of the Soviet Union brought hope to Tibetan independence advocates, who believed that just as Ukraine, Belarus, and Kazakhstan could become independent, so could Tibet. Of course all peoples have the right to self-determination. Although the Tibetan people are a minority nationality within China, they still have that right. Because many Chinese live in Tibetan areas outside the Tibet Autonomous Region (TAR), ethnic self-determination and independence would have an impact on relations in all the border regions surrounding Tibet. If such issues cannot be resolved, a serious border conflict or civil war will ensue. The disintegration of Czechoslovakia and of Yugoslavia are perfect examples of these two alternatives. The problem of Tibet's future, although it concerns the Tibetan people, also concerns all of China; consultation is needed on both sides to come to a resolution.

**The Tibet Autonomous Region and "Greater Tibet"**

The Tibetan territory has the highest altitudes in the world. Having an average altitude of more than 4,000 meters above sea level, it is known as the "roof of the world." The Tibet Autonomous Region (TAR) of the People's Republic of China and what the Dalai Lama calls the "entire Tibetan territory" are two different geographic areas. The TAR includes Lhasa and the six prefectures (*xingshu*) of Shigatse, Lhoka (Shannan), Nyingtri (Linzhi), Qamdo (Chamdo), Nagchu (Naqu), and Ngari—altogether seventy-six counties covering an area of more than 1.2 million square kilometers. Tibetans also occupy Inner Tibet, namely:

- Qinghai Province—Tsochang (Haibei), Malho (Huangnan), Golog, Yushu and Tsolho (Hainan) Tibetan autonomous prefectures, and in Tsonub (Haixi) Mongol-Tibetan-Kazak autonomous prefecture.
- Southern Gansu Province—Kanlho (Gannan) Tibetan autonomous prefecture and Pari (Tianzhu) Tibetan autonomous county.
- Western Sichuan Province—in Ngaba (Aba) and Kanze (Ganze) Tibetan autonomous prefectures, and in Muli Tibetan autonomous county.
- Northwestern Yunnan Province—in Deqen (Dechen) Tibetan autonomous prefecture.

So-called Greater Tibet is the same as what Tibetans call the "entire Tibetan territory" and consists of the TAR plus the Tibetan regions in Qinghai, Gansu, Sichuan and Yunnan. The Dalai Lama calls these regions "U-Tsang," "Kham," and "Amdo." The area of the "entire Tibetan territory" is roughly twice the size of the TAR. According to the fourth Chinese census at the beginning of the 1990s, 3.1 percent of Tibetans were in exile. The TAR's total population was 2,196,000, of which 2,096,000 were Tibetan, forming 95.46 percent of the TAR's total population and 43.35 percent of the total Tibetan population worldwide. More Tibetans are spread across Sichuan, Qinghai, Gansu, and Yunnan than live in the TAR—a total of 2,496,500, or 51.55 percent. But in these regions, Chinese and Tibetans, Mongols and Kazaks live together in the same areas. Because the number of Chinese domiciled within the TAR comprises less than 5 percent, what the Dalai Lama calls Chinese immigration to Tibet apparently refers to the Tibetan regions of Sichuan, Gansu, Qinghai, and Yunnan. Because of this unique demographic situation, a resolution of the Tibetan problem will have to be such that each nationality is able to accept the others.

**Three Alternatives for a Future Tibet**

There are countless alternatives regarding the issue of Tibet's future, but three are most viable:

1. Continuing the present system of the Tibet Autonomous Region;
2. Granting full Tibetan independence;
3. Establishing a federal system, in which Tibet is allowed to be more "autonomous" than regular provinces with the status of "special member state"; thus relations between Tibet and a federal China would resemble a confederation.

The present "autonomous" system is in reality a centralized system. According to the regulations of the "law on autonomy for minority nationality areas of the People's Republic of China," those who hold the posts of chairman of the autonomous region and chairman and vice chairman of the standing committee of the regional people's congress should come from the nationality of that region, and members of the regional government should, as far as possible, come from the nationality of the region. The autonomous region has the right to draw up autonomous and local regulations, to make changes in certain high-level decisions according to specific conditions, to set up a police force for the region, to enjoy the local culture, to publish in the local language, and to manage the region's administration.

But because China has a system of centralized power, these "autonomous rights" depend entirely on the whim of the central government. During the Cultural Revolution, such rights virtually ceased to exist. Only later, when the central government introduced more enlightened policies, were any autonomous rights seen again anywhere in China. Still, the thirty years since the creation of the TAR indicate that even though the chairman of the autonomous region and all the important posts of the autonomous region have been held by Tibetans, the candidates for these posts were all decided in Beijing. In short, what exists is a system where "autonomous rights" are subject to central government control and there are no safeguards.

Another option a future Tibet could choose is "Tibetan independence." The vast majority of Tibetans in exile advocate independence. Some Tibetan organizations consider it the long-term goal of their struggle and are dissatisfied with the Dalai

Lama's moderate position as set forth in Strasbourg. But among the exiled Tibetans, some are moderate supporters of independence who advocate resolving the Tibetan problem through compromise. Specifically they suggest deciding Tibet's future by means of a referendum of Tibetan citizens; if the majority did not agree with independence, these moderates would comply with that decision.

Some Tibetans within the TAR advocate independence; some oppose it. But the heavy-handed policies of the Chinese Communist Party mean that a considerable number of Tibetans do not dare reveal their true views publicly on the question of independence. Since the 1980s Tibetans' living standards have improved markedly. The vast majority of Tibetans have great respect for the Dalai Lama and hope that he will return to his homeland. Because living standards have been improving, some groups of Tibetans have little desire for independence. For more than forty years the CCP has cultivated Tibetan cadres in Tibet. Roughly thirty-eight thousand hold the administrative posts in the autonomous region and all the leadership posts at the county level and below. Thus a new social class of rich Tibetans is emerging. The vast majority of them do not support Tibetan independence. Further, more than eighteen thousand Tibetan technical cadres in Tibet do not generally support Tibetan independence. In Qinghai, Sichuan, and other provinces where the remaining 51 percent of the Tibetan population is concentrated, the Tibetans live placidly alongside Chinese, Mongols, Kazaks, and other nationalities. Among the generations born after 1949 the concept of "Greater Tibet" has yet to take shape, and the idea of Tibetan independence is extremely hazy.

In post-Deng China the rise of regionalism will be an irresistible trend, and the demand for Tibetan independence could increase. China has effected intermittently a system of centralized power for more than two thousand years, but on occasion there has been a power vacuum at the center, with loss of control over the regions and the country breaking up. If, in post-Deng China, Tibet declares independence, then independence movements might also break out in Xinjiang and Inner Mongolia. At present, however, such a scenario is impossible to predict. We cannot even speculate as to whether, if China were to disintegrate in this manner, there would be peaceful coexistence or a long, drawn-out civil war in the style of Yugoslavia.

## Resolution of the Tibetan Problem on the Basis of a Federal System

In post-Deng China the prospect of Taiwanese independence exists as well as that of Tibetan independence. The Taiwan and Tibet questions have obvious differences. Currently the "Republic of China" on Taiwan is actually independent from the "People's Republic of China" on the mainland. Unlike Taiwan, the TAR and other Tibetan areas are de facto part of the PRC, and Tibetan independence would involve an actual breakup of China, whereas independence for Taiwan would simply be a matter of changing the country's name.

A federal system would be a good alternative for a future Greater China. Such a step would (1) effectively safeguard the nation's territory; (2) promote the development and progress of each nationality and region; (3) avert the possibility of interminable warfare as a result of China's disintegration; and (4) bring about the peaceful unification of Taiwan [and mainland China] on the basis of equality.

Federalism is a kind of national structure, and whether one country or several are involved, the system would have the same problems as that of a "national structure." National structure is a problem of relations between the country as a whole and its various components, and between the central government and the regional governments. National structure can take two forms; it can be a simple system or a compound system. In the former, a division exists between centralized power and the local distribution of power. The compound system can be either a federation or a confederation. (The "personal union" compound form has also emerged in history.)

A federation is an integrated country made up of many united members (republics, states, prefectures, or regions). The federation has the highest legislative and administrative bodies as well as a unified constitution and legal code. In international relations the federation exercises the primary power over foreign affairs. Each member of the federation (who could be designated "member states") has its respective constitution and legal codes, and each has its respective legislative, administrative, and judicial bodies. The division of authority between the federation and its member states would generally be stipulated in explicit terms by the federal constitution.

Another pattern for creating a compound national structure is the confederation, whereby several independent countries, in terms of defense and economic policies, organize into a "national" alliance/union for purposes of economics or defense. The confederation is not the main organ for international relations, nor does it have the highest legislative bodies or a united army, tax system, budget, or citizenship. A "confederal parliament" or a summit conference links the confederation and its member states. The confederation's member states are actual countries, each with full legislative, diplomatic, military, administrative, and budgetary powers.

In a future China, taking into account the particular characteristics of Taiwan and Tibet, the Dalai Lama's various positions on the problem of Tibet's future, and the status of Hong Kong and Macao, a federal system for a future China would have to take on a new form, such as a "federation with the form of a confederation," in order to allow Taiwan, Tibet, and other regions' relations with the federation to have "confederal" characteristics. To this end, a future Chinese federation could be divided into two kinds of "member states"—such as regular member states and member states with special characteristics. The member states with such special characteristics would be Taiwan, Xinjiang, Inner Mongolia, Guangxi, Ningxia, Hong Kong, and Macao. The regular member states would include Beijing, Shanghai, and Tianjin and Hebei, Heilongjiang, Sichuan, Guangdong, and the other provinces.

Thus were China to be organized as a federation, Tibet would be a "member state with special characteristics" and a number of important differences would emerge compared to the present "autonomous region." Some of these are as follows:

- Tibet would draw up a constitution or basic law to set up the nature and powers of its government structure and to safeguard the freedom and rights of the Tibetan people, including religious freedom;
- The immediate source of power of the Tibetan member state's government would come from the people of all of Tibet, not from the federal government alone. The federal government would have no power under any circumstances to dismiss or replace different levels of officials in the Tibetan member state's government.
- The Tibetan state could maintain and develop economic and cultural relations with other countries and regions and with relevant international organizations; it also could conclude and sign relevant agreements with the name "Tibet, China" (*Zhongguo Xizang*).
- In internal affairs, the Tibetan member state would have full power to make independent decisions and would have the independence to maintain public finances.
- The Tibetan member state would have legislative power in accordance with the constitution of the Tibetan member state or the legislation of Tibet's basic law, and would not need the approval of the federal parliament to put any law into effect.
- The Tibetan member state, in judicial terms, would have a supreme court.
- The Tibetan member state would fly both the federal and member state's flag; thus the snow lion flag would again become a legal flag in Tibet.
- The federal government would not be able to put forced population transfer policies into practice in Tibet. All inhabitants originally from the interior who were willing to return

to the interior would have the power to do so. However, federal China would be a united country, and the Tibetan state would not be able to forbid people from other regions from coming to live and work in Tibet of their own volition. The Tibetans would likewise have the right to live and work in other regions of a federal China.
- All other autonomous powers of the former TAR—[the right] to organize the region's police force, the right to use and develop the Tibetan language and culture, and so forth—would exist under the federal system.

To give expression to the characteristics of a "federation with the form of a confederation" in a future federal China, the federal parliament would be able to establish two houses. One (designated the "federal house") would reflect and represent the interests of each member state. But in order to enable Tibet, Taiwan, and the other member states with special characteristics to have greater influence in the federal house, the member states with special characteristics could hold more seats than the regular member states. In the other house of the federal parliament, each member state, including Tibet, would be able to draft any kind of federal legislation. Under the present unitary system, the central government can, when it chooses, hold up a certain procedure and withdraw a regional government's powers. Under the federal system, the federal government's powers would not be so sweeping, and the scope of the federation's powers and those of each member state would be set down in the federal constitution, to which Tibet, Taiwan, and the other member states would all have agreed.

In a future federal China the border of the Tibetan member state would retain at least what is now the TAR. As for whether it would also include Inner Tibet, the federation would establish a special committee to delineate the border on the basis of peaceful consultation. The federal parliament would ultimately decide the scope of the Tibetan border and other border changes.

The "confederal federation" would be a new kind of "federation." Because of the special status of Tibet, Taiwan, and other special member states, the federal constitution would have to list their special rights on the basis of "special provisions." In a confederal form of federation, the federal constitution would also have to stipulate that these "special provisions" could not be altered without being approved in the legislative bodies of Tibet, Taiwan, and so forth.

The "confederal federation" would offer a new alternative for a future Tibet and a future China that would remove all kinds of problems stemming from the centralization of power over each region and that would provide an opportunity for the comprehensive development of each region and of the people's imaginations. Each region could produce its own plans and measures in accordance with its own circumstances and adopt measures suitable for the region in accordance with that region's culture and actual circumstances. This kind of federal system would not only help to maintain a lasting peace between each region but would help produce regional development for a multicultural China. Tibet would have freedom, democracy, cultural and religious liberty, and sound environmental practices.

The federal system is a nonviolent road. Before organizing a federation, all China's component parts and all its political forces would have to hold bilateral and multilateral talks on each aspect of a future China. In terms of the country as a whole, they would also have to discuss and develop the form of the national structure in the future China—a system with centralized power or one with developing power, a federal system or a confederal system. If these forces could get together and discuss a balanced proposal, perhaps it would find acceptance. But this proposal, before being accepted, would still have to be approved by the committee drawing up the constitution.

## Notes

1. The Dalai Lama on Capital Hill (Washington, D.C.): "Five-point Peace Plan" on the future of Tibet, September 21, 1987.

2. The Dalai Lama, in an interview with parliamentarians and journalists at the European Parliament in Strasbourg, France, June 15, 1988.
3. Ibid.
4. Ibid.
5. The Dalai Lama, in an interview with *New York Newsday*: "Hoping for a Democratic China"; cited in *The World Journal*, May 1, 1994, A16.
6. "Tibetan Government-in-Exile Declares the Invalidity of the Strasbourg Proposal," *Tibet Forum*, March 1992.

# Two Focuses of the Tibet Issue

## Yiu Yung-Chin

Arguments over the Tibet issue revolve around two questions: First, has Tibet belonged to China historically? Second, for the past forty years, on balance has the Chinese Communist government brought Tibetans benefit or harm?

The Chinese government insists that the answer to the first question is yes and that benign rule in Tibet has enhanced the legitimacy of its rule there.

Before China's Tang dynasty (618–907), Tibet had almost no relations with China. The Tibet-China relationship during the Tang dynasty was clearly nation-state to nation-state. Princess Wen Cheng's marriage to Tibetan king Songtsan Gampo illustrates such a relationship. Of course we cannot conclude that because China and Tibet were two countries during the Tang dynasty, so too must they be two countries today.

The territory controlled by China's Song dynasty (960–1126) was even smaller than the Tang's had been, and Tibet was not included in it. The Mongol's Yuan dynasty (1271–1368) did occupy Tibet, but we must keep in mind that it was the *Mongols* who conquered Tibet (as they did China). It is far-fetched to claim China's sovereignty over Tibet on this history.

The territory of the Ming dynasty (1368–1644) was confined to the Han-occupied areas; that is, China was bound by the Great Wall on the North (with occasional control of Inner Mongolia). To the West, China included only Gansu, Sichuan, and Yunnan. The Ming did not possess Tibet. True, the Manchus, who conquered China in 1644, brought Tibet under their suzerainty in

1720. Their "Qing dynasty" also included all of Mongolia. This bit of history provides some basis for the Chinese government's claim that "Tibet has been part of China historically." However, the way the Qing Court treated Tibet and Mongolia was quite different from the way it treated other frontier provinces that it had conquered, such as Xinjiang, Yunnan, and Taiwan. Many historical documents demonstrate that Mongolia and Tibet were protectorates, which means that, unlike the other provinces of China, Tibet and Mongolia were not directly subordinate to the Qing Court. Tibet and Mongolia were special administrative divisions; they had total autonomy over their domestic affairs.

Granted, the Qing (Manchu) dynasty had an army stationed in Tibet. But that does not necessarily mean that China thereby gained sovereign rights to Tibet. The United States also has armies stationed in many Asian and European countries for the purpose of protection only.

The Chinese also argue that China's central government was involved in choosing the reincarnations of the Dalai Lama and the Panchen Lama. But this was a symbolic involvement. The Chinese had no right to vote either yes or no.

Therefore, until the end of the Manchu dynasty, both the Qing Court and the Chinese people regarded Tibet and China as separate. The Qing Court never required Tibetans to pledge loyalty to Qing emperors. The Tibetan people recognized only the Tibetan government led by Dalai Lama. In fact the so-called Tibet-China relationship was strictly between the heads of Qing and Tibetan governments.

The Republican authorities (Nationalists) were never able to maintain forces in Tibet. Thus for a time Tibet was de facto independent. Only in the early 1950s did the Chinese begin to exercise control in Tibet and make Tibet subordinate like other Chinese provinces. The Chinese Communist army took over Tibet by military force and stripped the Tibetans' sovereign rights to their own country. Now we should ask: What has the Chinese Communist government done for Tibet?

According to the Chinese government's propaganda, before

the Communists took over Tibet, the Tibetans had been no better than "beasts of burden." The government has propagandized to the Chinese about how a small group of Tibetan serf owners not only exploited the serfs but tortured them ruthlessly—by skinning them alive, pulling out their tendons, and pouring hot oil on their bodies. We now know these are brazen lies. Overall, the relationship between landlord and tenant-peasant in Tibet was better than in China. There were incidents in China where peasants were beaten to death or female tenants were raped by landlords, but such episodes of course cannot epitomize all China civilization. So why should a few extreme cases in Tibet represent the entire Tibetan situation?

Indeed only after the Communists took over were oppression, execution, and torture so prevalent. Even Hu Yaobang, former general secretary of the Chinese Communist Party, once said that the (Chinese) government's conduct in Tibet resembled that of the colonialists. It might be added that inasmuch as the government had treated the Chinese so badly, one can hardly expect them to treat Tibetans, long the victims of Chinese discrimination, any better.

There is only one way to solve the Tibetan problem: the Han Chinese must repent for what they did in Tibet.

# Contributors

*Cao Changching.* Cao was deputy editor-in-chief of the outspoken newspaper *Shenzhen Youth Journal,* which was shut down by the Chinese authorities in 1987 after it published a series of dissidents' articles and called on Deng Xiaoping to retire. He came to the United States in 1988 and the next year founded *Press Freedom Herald,* the first such newspaper run by dissident Chinese journalists. He served as the paper's editor-in-chief from 1989 to 1990. Cao has been research fellow at the East Asian Institute of Columbia University in New York, and at the Institute of Culture and Communications of East-West Center in Honolulu. Cao has published about four hundred essays, poems, reports and, feature stories both in and out of China. He is coauthor of four Chinese-language books: *Modern Chinese Poetry Study, Avante Garde Poetry of Modern China, Voices of Dissent in the Chinese Media: Seeds of Democracy,* and *Chinese Intellectual's View on the Tibet Issue.* He has been a columnist of *Open Magazine* (Hong Kong) since 1995.

*Ding Zilin.* Ding is assistant professor of The People's University of China in Beijing. Aside from coauthoring a book on aesthetics in ancient Greece (see under Jiang Peikun), she published the provocative *Name List of Victims of The June 4 Massacre.* The only son of Jiang Peikun and Ding Zilin was killed in the June 4, 1989, massacre.

*Fang Lizhi.* An astrophysicist, Fang has been a member of the Chinese Academy of Sciences, as well as a professor and the vice president of the China's University of Science and Technology. In 1987 he was accused by the Chinese government of promoting "bourgeois liberalization" and was discharged from the university. In June 1989 he felt compelled to seek sanctuary in the U.S. Embassy in Beijing, where he remained for thirteen months before being allowed to proceed to the United States. Since then he has been active in human rights causes and has served on advisory committees for many human rights organizations. Since 1992 he has been a professor of physics and astronomy at the University of Arizona.

*Jiang Peikun.* Professor Jiang specialized in aesthetics at The People's University of China in Beijing. He is the author of the book *Aesthetic Activities* (in Chinese), and coauthor (with Ding Zilin) of *Aesthetics and Poetry of Ancient Greece.*

*Seymour, James D.* Research Scholar at Columbia University, Seymour is the author of numerous articles and books about Chinese and Tibetan affairs. He is coauthor of *New Ghosts, Old Ghosts: Prisons and Labor Reform Camps in China* (1997).

*Shen Tong.* For his leadership role in the Tiananmen student demonstrations, *Newsweek* declared Shen one of its "Persons of the Year" for 1989. He is the author of *Almost a Revolution*, which has appeared in English, French, and Japanese. He is now a Ph.D. candidate at Boston University.

*Song Liming.* Long interested in Tibetan history, Song was once a Ph.D. candidate in international relations at the Department of History at Nanjing University. He left China in 1989 and entered the Political Sciences Institute of Florence University in Italy as a visiting scholar.

*Wang Ruowang.* A prominent writer, Wang used to be deputy chief editor of *Shanghai Literature Monthly.* In 1957 he was arrested and sentenced to four years in jail for speaking out against Mao's policy in 1957. In the 1980s he criticized Deng Xiaoping's reforms for being limited to economics and in 1987 was expelled from the Communist Party along with two other well-known dissidents, Fang Lizhi and Liu Binyan. Beginning in 1989 he spent fourteen months in prison for his support and involvement in the recent democracy movement. Wang came to the United Sates in 1993 as a visiting scholar at the East Asian Institute of Columbia University. One of his books, *Hunger Trilogy*, was translated into English and published by M. E. Sharpe in 1991. He now lives in New York.

*Wei Jingsheng.* An electrician by trade, Wei was a leading activist and essayist in the 1979 "Democracy Wall" movement. He argued that in addition to Deng Xiaoping's policy of Four Modernizations, China needs a "fifth modernization," namely, political modernization based on democracy and rule of law. Since then he has almost continuously been in prison.

*Wu, Harry.* After criticizing the Communist Party and speaking out against the Soviet invasion of Hungary, Wu was arrested and imprisoned for many years as a "counterrevolutionary rightist." He came to the United States in 1985. His books *Laogai—The Chinese Gulag* and *Bitter Winds* tell this story. In the summer of 1995 he returned to the PRC and was arrested on grounds that he had illegally entered the country. He was convicted of "stealing state secrets" and sentenced to fifteen years, but instead was immediately expelled from China. Wu is Executive Director of the Laogai Research Foundation, and a Research Fellow at the Hoover Institution of Stanford University.

*Xiang Xiaoji.* In 1989, when a graduate student at the Chinese University of Political Science and Law in Beijing, Xiang acted as a Coordinator of Beijing College Students Dialogue Delegation during the Tiananmen democracy movement. He escaped to the United States after the Beijing massacre, and enrolled in the Law School of Columbia University. He is now with a New York law firm.

*Xue Wei.* Before coming to the United States in 1980, Xue served ten years imprisonment as a "counterrevolutionary." In recent years he has been involved in the overseas Chinese democracy movement and is currently the associate editor and manager of *Beijing Spring* magazine.

*Yan Jiaqi.* Director of the Political Science Institute of the Institute of Social Sciences of China from 1982 to 1989, Yan was involved in the abortive 1989 pro-democracy movement in Beijing and then escaped abroad. From September 1989 to September 1990 he was chairman of the Federation for a Democratic China. He was a visiting scholar at the Human Rights Center of Columbia University from 1993 to 1994. Yan published fifteen books in China, some of which were translated into English. The latest English translation of his work is *Turbulent Decade—A History of The Cultural Revolution* (coauthored with Gao Gao). He is presently a freelance writer living in New York.

*Yiu Yung-chin.* A student at Shanghai's Fudan University when the 1989 democracy movement unfolded, Yiu then became a leader of the Shanghai Student Federation. He was subsequently arrested and jailed for a year. He is now studying economics at the University of California, Los Angeles.

# Index

Altan Khan, 7
Amnesty International, 12
*Atlas of Chinese History Maps, The*, 93
Avedon, John F., xiii, 26

Bell, Charles, 58-59
Bhutan, 88
*Biographies of the Dalai Lamas* (Ya Hanzhang), 6-7, 25
Britain, 20, 57, 58-59, 76, 79, 80, 81
Bulag, U.E., xxvin.1

Cao Changching, xiii, xiv, xviii, xxiv, xxvi, 3-30, 125
Chen Duxiu, 17
Chiang Ching-kuo, 94
Chiang Kai-shek, xxv, 5-6, 7-8, 94
China-Tibet relations
  historical, xvi-xix, 3-11, 86, 92, 93-95, 100, 110-111, 121-122
  *See also* Independence movement; Tibet, Chinese rule in
Chinese Revolution of 1911, 58, 94
Ci Xi, 4

Collective values, Chinese, 17-18, 29, 33
Commune system, 71
Cue Rengui, 86
Cultural Revolution, xiv, 31, 64, 71-72, 107, 113
Czechoslovakia, self-determination rights in, 74, 111

Dalai Lama, xv-xvi, 37, 82, 107, 116
  Chinese propaganda about, 26-27
  creation of title, 6-7
  enthronement of Fourteenth, 6, 7-8
  flight to India, 31, 62-63, 73
  government-in-exile, 21, 30, 98, 104-105
  on human rights abuses, 13
  nonviolence of, 73, 108
  and peaceful coexistence, 52
  in peace negotiations, 20, 64, 65, 85, 88, 108-109, 113-114
  and Qing dynasty, 8, 10, 78-79
  reincarnation of, 99, 122
  and Seventeen-point agreement, 55, 57, 61, 72

*129*

## 130   INDEX

Dalai Lama *(continued)*
  Thirteenth, 4, 5, 58, 59
  and Tiananmen demonstration, 32, 41-42
  Deng Xiaoping, xxii, 11, 29, 62, 64, 94
  Wei Jingsheng's letter to, 75-88, 91
"Destroy the olds" campaign, xiv
Ding Zilin, 31-35, 125
Divorce law, 97-98
Domino theory, xxii, xxiii-xxiv, 15-17
Dong Xianguang, 8
Dzungar Mongol rebellion, 77

Economy, Tibetan, 13-14, 34, 87, 95, 114

Fang Lizhi, 37-40, 125-126
*Farewell Party, The* (Kundera), 29
Federal system, xii, 113, 115-119
Four Modernizations, 91
Friere, Paulo, xiv

Gampo, Songsten, King, xvi, 3, 5, 6, 92, 121
Gansu, viii, xii, 112
Genghis Khan, 4, 6
Golden Urn Lottery System, 76
Gompo, Songtsen, xvi
Great Leap Forward, 83
Guangdong, 116
Guangxi, 116
Guomindang, xxiv, 7-8, 56, 81-82, 122
Gyatso, Sonam, 7
Hebei, 116
Heilongjiang, 116

Helsinki Accord, 16
Hong Kong, xx, xxii, 62, 67, 97, 98, 116
Huang Musong, 56
Human rights abuses, xxi, 12-13, 28, 31-32, 42-45, 64, 95-96, 123
Hu Yaobang, 13, 32, 65, 107

Independence movement, xv
  *vs* collective values, 17-18, 29, 33
  comparison to other movements, 98
  Dalai Lama and, 20, 52, 65, 85, 88, 108-109, 113-114
  federal system alternative to, xii, 113, 115-119
  liberal principle and, 48-50
  national disintegration fears and, xxii, xxiii-xxiv, 15-17, 96, 97-98, 100, 114-115
  national security fears and, 19-20, 100
  non-Tibetan population and, 50-51
  self-determination rights and, xx-xxi, xxiv-xxv, 18-19, 22, 33, 34-35, 38, 74, 103-104
  Soviet example and, 15, 16, 74, 83-84, 111
  Tibetan view of, xxii-xxiii, 113-114
  unification principle *vs* freedom principle and, 100-101, 104
  viability of independent Tibet, 20-22, 33-34
India, 80, 81, 88

India *(continued)*
  independence of, 58-59, 82
  Tibetan exiles in, 21, 29-30,
    62-63, 104-105, 107
  and Tibetan independence, 19, 20
*In Exile from the Land of Snows*
  (Avedon), 26

Jiang Peikun, 31-35, 126
Jiang Ping, 69n.13
Jigme Ngapo, 72

Kang Youwei, 17
Kublai Khan, 4
Kundera, Milan, xiv, 29

Lee Teng-hui, 94
Lenin, 100
Liang Qichao, 17
Liang Shuming, 17
Lian Yu, 59
Liu Bocheng, 76
Lu You, 92

Macao, 116
Manchus. *See* Qing dynasty
Mao Zedong, xxv, 29, 30, 61, 82,
  93, 94, 95
Ming dynasty, xvii, 4, 94, 121
*Modern History of Tibet* (Xizang
  Fengun Lu), 25
Monasteries, destruction of, xiv,
  14, 31, 71-72
Mongol Empire, 4, 5, 6, 93, 100, 121
Mongolia, 93, 115, 116, 122
Nationalism
  Chinese, 17, 22, 26, 29,
    43, 73

Nationalism *(continued)*
  dark side of, 39
  minority, 38-39
Neo-authoritarian doctrine, 17-18
Nepal, 57, 76, 88, 107
Ngapo Ngawang Jigme, 8
Ningxia, 116
Nobel Peace Prize, 73

Panchen Lama, 12, 31, 55, 57,
  73, 98, 122
Phagpa, Grand Lama, 4
Potomac Conference, xiv-xv, xx,
  xxiii
Poverty, 13
Prejudice, anti-Tibetan, 15, 85-87
Propaganda, Chinese, xiii-xiv,
  25-30, 32, 73, 85, 92-93,
  99-100, 123
Puerto Rico, and
  self-determination, 18-19

Qing dynasty (Manchus),
  xvii-xviii, 4, 5, 6-7, 8, 10-11,
  58, 77-79, 94, 95, 110-111,
  121-122
Qinghai, viii, xii, xviii, 112, 114
Red Guards, 72
Religious persecution, 14, 28, 31,
  71-72, 88, 95
Ren Rong, 13

Self-determination rights, xx-xxi,
  xxiv-xxv, 18-19, 22, 33,
  34-35, 38, 74, 83-84, 103-104
Seventeen-point Agreement,
  xviii, 5, 55-67, 72
Seymour, James D., xi-xxvi, 126
Shen Tong, 41-53, 126

Shen Ts'ung-lien, 59
Sichuan, viii, xii, 110, 112, 114, 116
Sikkim, 88
Simla Convention of 1914, 57, 58, 80
Snow, Edgar, xxv
Song dynasty, 4, 121
Song Liming, 55-67, 126
Soviet Union, self-determination rights in, 15, 16, 74, 83-84, 111
Strasbourg Proposal, 65, 67, 69n.20, 70n.21, 109
Sun-Joffe Manifesto, xxiv
Sun Yat-sen, xviii, xxiv, 4, 94
Taiwan, xx, 61-62, 67, 97, 98, 116, 122
Takla, Phuntsok Tashi, xviii
Tang Daxian, 12-13
Tang dynasty, xvi, xxvin.9, 3, 5, 6, 92, 121
Thirteenth Laogai Farm, 91-92
Thonden, Phintso, xx
Thurman, Robert, 21
Tiananmen demonstrations, xiv, 17, 32
Tianjin, 116
Tibet
  Chinese representative (Amban) in, 76-77
  and Guomindang, 5-6, 7-8, 56, 81-82, 122
  independent, 4-5, 11, 58-59, 60-61, 77, 79-81, 93
  in Mongol Empire, 4, 5, 6, 93, 100, 121
  and Qing dynasty, 4, 5, 6-7, 8, 10-11, 58, 77-79, 94-95, 110-111, 121-122

Tibet *(continued)*
  serfdom in, 20-21, 33-34, 82, 99, 123
  and Tang dynasty, xvi, 3, 5, 6, 92, 121
  Tibetans in exile, 20, 21, 29-30, 62-63, 104-105, 112
  *See also* Dalai Lama
Tibet, Chinese rule in
  assimilation and, 50
  centralized power and, 113, 114
  Chinese dissident attitudes toward, 43-47, 103-105
  Chinese population and, 50-51, 112
  commune system under, 71
  democracy movement and, 45-47
  economic deprivations under, 13-14, 34, 87, 95
  Greater Tibet, viii, 112, 114
  human rights abuses of, xxi, 12-13, 28, 31-32, 42-45, 64, 95-96, 107, 123
  Inner Tibet, viii, xii, xviii, 111-112
  integration principle and, 51-53
  international recognition of Chinese claim, xix
  leftist policies and, 83
  legitimacy of Chinese claim, xi-xii, xv-xx, 4, 5-11
  1959 revolt against, 12, 31, 41, 62-63, 73, 83, 107, 108
  political repression under, 12, 28, 31, 41, 62, 107
  Potomac Conference on, xiv-xv, xx

Tibet *(continued)*
  propaganda about, xiii-xiv, 11-12, 25-30, 32, 33, 73, 85, 92-93, 99-100, 123
  racial discrimination under, 15, 85-87
  reformist policy and, 108
  religious persecution under, 14, 28, 31, 71-72, 88, 95
  Seventeen-point Agreement and, xviii, 5, 55-67, 72
  Tibetan cadres and, 114
  Tibet Autonomous Region (TAR), vii-viii, xviii, 13, 74, 111-112
  voluntary unity and, 76-85
  White Paper on, 11-12, 20-21, 73, 75, 76, 77, 80, 87
  *See also* Independence movement
Treaty of 821, 55
Tu-bo kingdom, xvi

United Nations Human Rights Commission, xxi
United States
  and Puerto Rico, 19
  recognition of Chinese claim, xix, xxi

Wanggyal, Phuntsog, 76, 82
Wang Ruouwang, 71-74, 127
Wan Li, 108

Wei Jingsheng, xx, xxiv, 15, 32, 75-88, 91, 127
Wen Cheng, Princess, xvi, 3, 5, 6, 86, 92, 121
Wen Zongyao, 59
White Paper, 11-12, 20, 73, 75, 76, 77, 80, 87
Wu, Harry, 91-96, 127
Wu Zhongxin, 6, 7-8

Xiang Xiaoji, 97-101, 127-128
Xinjiang, 115, 116, 122
Xizang Fengun Lu, 25
Xu Bangtai, xv-xvi, xvii
Xue Wei, 103-105, 128
Xu Mingxu, 27-29, 30

Ya Hanzhang, xiii, 6-7, 10, 25, 76, 82
Yan Fu, 17
Yan Jiaqi, xii, 107-119, 128
Yin Fatang, 13
Yiu Yung-Chin, 121-123, 128
Yuan dynasty, xiii, xvi, xvii, 5, 6, 93, 100, 121
Yue Fei, 92-93
Yugoslavia, self-determination rights and, 83, 84, 111
Yunnan, viii, 112, 122

Zhang Taiyan, 17
Zhao Erfeng, 110-111
Zhu Yuanzhang, xviii